"*Friendship Can Save the World* off[...] the reader enter the biblical narrative of Ruth to discern wisdom for living within our highly polemical, polarized society. Morgan and Carrie Stephens are master storytellers who relate the book of Ruth to their own experience leading a multicultural church. The title says it all. God welcomes us. How can we not share friendship with diverse others? It might even save the world. I highly recommend this book for churches and individuals."

—**Gregg Okesson,** PhD, Provost and Senior Vice President for Academic Affairs, Asbury Theological Seminary, author of *A Public Missiology*

"I thought I knew the story of Ruth, but *Friendship Can Save the World* reveals a much bigger picture of God's redemptive plan when the paths of law and love converge. Carrie and Morgan openly share how a diverse church can flourish when mirroring the multiethnic and multigenerational friendship Ruth and Naomi had. This hard and beautiful gospel-based clinging produces the very community our collective souls long for."

—**Jodi Grubbs,** slow-living advocate and podcast host

"Wow, I'll never see the book of Ruth the same again! *Friendship Can Save the World* is a beautiful apologetic for multiethnic, multigenerational relationships in Christian faith communities. This book gives us a gospel-centered systematic defense for relational unity in a faith-world filled with homogenous preferences. Carrie and Morgan provide us with real stories and actionable steps to push through relational pain points so that we, together, can choose to love like Jesus—sacrificially."

—**Rosalynn Smith,** PhD, author of *A Prayer for Baby*

"By amplifying multiethnic and multigenerational voices, Carrie and Morgan Stephens guide us into a diverse and meaningful community. As they walk us through the book of Ruth, they help us discover common ground in our faith and teach us how to build friendships instead of walls. Churches will benefit from the humility and wisdom in the pages of this book!"

—**Stephanie Gilbert,** author and cohost of the *Pastors' Wives Tell All* podcast

"Morgan and Carrie have skillfully crafted a literary tapestry that intertwines everyday relational fibers with those of the iconic Old Testament saint Ruth. Every turn of the page encourages you to be more to those who need more."

—**Brett Fuller,** Bishop, Grace Covenant Church, Washington Metropolitan Area and Chaplain, Washington Commanders

"True friendship does not come without vulnerability, because there will be times when challenges make friendship seem one-sided. This book helps us bridge that gap with authentic personal stories and a beautiful link to a strong biblical story. If we choose to become vulnerable and allow the stories to speak to our own weaknesses, hurts, anger, and judgements, we will grow as friends and, so, save the world through our friendship with Christ as our first friend."

—**Pierre Ferreira,** Senior Pastor, Every Nation, George, South Africa

"Martin Luther King Jr. once said, 'We must learn to live together as brothers and sisters or perish together as fools.' Offering itself as more than just a book but also a brilliant invitation, *Friendship Can Save the World* brings us more into what it truly means to live together as brothers and sisters, and more into what Jesus meant when he offers the fullness of life. Through stories of pain and delight infused with hard-won wisdom, Carrie and Morgan masterfully display the sobering reality of the great sacrifice paired with the invaluable reward that accompanies this life. After reading you will leave with a refreshed view of the Father's heart to see the dividing wall of hostility crumble and the part we play in seeing that happen."

—**Adrian Crawford,** Founding Pastor, Engage Church Tallahassee, author of *Mask Off*

"While the themes of this book are familiar to us, Carrie and Morgan explore them with a touch that's brave, intentional, and sensitive. Diversity not for its own sake but for God's glory. Friendship that pushes past the pain into glory. Redemption that can restore the most hopeless situations. I appreciated their humility in being vulnerable with their stories, as well as giving a platform to a number of voices who enrich and validate their message."

—**Joseph Bonifacio,** pastor, author, online content creator

"Carrie and Morgan are great leaders, great Christians, and great at relational leadership. Together, they will guide you through Ruth's journey of loss and love as she came to find faith in the context of friendship—redemption in the midst of relationship. In a relationally famished world, these words will be like water to the soul."

—**Adam Mabry,** Senior Pastor of Aletheia Church, author of *When God Seems Gone, Stop Taking Sides*, and *The Art of Rest*

FRIENDSHIP CAN SAVE THE WORLD

FRIENDSHIP CAN SAVE THE WORLD

The Book of Ruth and the Power
of Diverse Gospel Community

CARRIE & MORGAN STEPHENS

LEAFWOOD
PUBLISHERS
an imprint of Abilene Christian University Press

FRIENDSHIP CAN SAVE THE WORLD

The Book of Ruth and the Power of Diverse Gospel Community

LEAFWOOD
P U B L I S H E R S
an imprint of Abilene Christian University Press

Copyright © 2023 by Carrie and Morgan Stephens

ISBN 978-1-68426-264-9

Printed in the United States of America

Published in association with Books & Such Literary Management, 52 Mission Circle, Suite 122, PMB 170, Santa Rosa, CA 95409-5370, www.booksandsuch.com.

Cataloging-in-Publication Data is on file at the Library of Congress, Washington, DC.

Cover design by Greg Jackson, Thinkpen Design | Interior text design by Sandy Armstrong, Strong Design

Leafwood Publishers is an imprint of Abilene Christian University Press.

ACU Box 29138 | Abilene, Texas 79699

1-877-816-4455 | www.leafwoodpublishers.com

23 24 25 26 27 28 29 / 7 6 5 4 3 2 1

For all who cling on the long road home.

CONTENTS

FOR THE LOVE OF RUTH

If you've peeked at the photo on the back of this book, you may wonder what two middle-age, middle-class, White pastors could know about diversity. It's a valid question.

Frankly, that question has kept us up at night for many years now because, for reasons only God knows, he has blessed us with the privilege of loving and serving a vibrant, diverse congregation of people with whom we often have little in common.

We write this book not as people who have a lived experience on the underside of racism, classism, or ageism, but as witnesses who have seen God do the impossible: bring many different people together and teach them how to love one another as friends.

In this book, you will hear stories of friendships that have saved people from all kinds of pain and suffering. These stories mirror an ancient book in the Old Testament about how God often clothes his rescue and provision in humanity's willingness to befriend one another, no matter the cost. The book of Ruth has taught us that one person's fiery love can ignite the hearts of a family, neighborhood, office, school, city, or even nation.

Our own love for Ruth began in the wake of the 2016 election. At that time, we had been lead pastors of Mosaic, a diverse church in Austin, Texas, for five years. Social media had changed a great deal since the 2012 election, and as the 2016 election tension built, many people took their fear and aggressive opinions to Facebook and Twitter. As a diverse church full of passionate people who don't always agree, we all learned together in that election how easily relationships within a church can be damaged by words posted or tweeted online.

In the middle of all this, God led us to the book of Ruth as a way to forge holy unity among people of different generations, races, political affiliations, and socioeconomic backgrounds. At its core, the book of Ruth tells an incredible story about the power of the friendships shared by Ruth, Naomi, and Boaz, who shared little in common apart from their faith in God. As some people in our church cheered the election results while others wept over them, we asked everyone to consider how their relationships reflected the gospel-centered message of these words Ruth spoke: "Where you go I will go, and where you stay I will stay. Your people will be my people and your God my God" (Ruth 1:16 NIV).

As we have clung to God and his people through the pain caused by difficult presidential elections, deep personal losses, and the disruption caused by a worldwide pandemic, we have gleaned friendships not rooted in cultural commonalities but in the friendship God offers us in himself.

We hope the stories and biblical teaching in this book help birth diverse and sacrificial friendships that fill the world with Christ's love.

But because we live in the world we do, allow us also a moment to be vulnerable. We haven't gotten everything right when it comes to building diverse communities and friendships, though we believe that we, through a lot of pain and trial and error and by God's grace, have stumbled onto some truths that work.

We are not trying to get you or your church to be like us. Sincerely. Please be who God made you to be, because as Catherine of Siena said, that's how we set the world on fire.[1]

We are not trying to push a cultural agenda on anyone. Instead, we will do our best to explore how the Bible doesn't support a singular cultural narrative or political agenda but asks all Christians to wrestle with how a proper theological awareness of salvation, conversion, justice, and discipleship intersects with our cultural approach to things like diversity, poverty, racism, privilege, and prejudice.

As we walk through the book of Ruth together, if you find the intersection of the gospel and our culture painful, we hope it is because your heart grieves for all the ways humans, especially Christian people, have been pulled apart and made into enemies when they could be friends.

If you would, forgive us where we fail and cheer us where we succeed in these pages. (That's what friends are for, right?)

We believe our human friendships can save the world when they are rooted in the divine friendship God has offered us through his Son, and we believe the book of Ruth is a gift that can light the way on the long road home together.

Deep breath.

Here goes.

---

[1] "Setting the World on Fire: Inspiring Quotes from St. Catherine of Siena," Archdiocese of Baltimore, April 29, 2014, https://www.archbalt.org/setting-the-world-on-fire-inspiring-quotes-from-st-catherine-of-siena/.

Chapter 1

A PROPHETIC VISION

Going All the Way to the Top

Salmon the father of Boaz, whose mother was Rahab, Boaz the father of Obed, whose mother was Ruth, Obed the father of Jesse, and Jesse the father of King David.

—Matt. 1:5–6 NIV

The book of Ruth is a gem of a story that has carried us personally, and our church at large, through many storms throughout the last decade. It's a story of people battered by trauma and loss. It's a story of people hungry for literal food and also starving for redemption. There are plot twists galore, some sketchy side characters, incredible townspeople, and a love story to boot. It's like *The Grapes of Wrath* meets *The Wild Wild West* meets *How Stella Got Her Groove Back*, all right inside the pages of God's Word. Yes, the book of Ruth offers us all of this and more in a tale of risk and reward that centers on what humanity needs more than ever right now: friendship.

The Hebrew narrative of Ruth tells the tale of the friendship of two women: a young pagan immigrant and an aging Jewish matriarch, who forge an unbreakable bond against all odds. Their story shows us how friendship and faith can sweep people up into the grand narrative of God's great story. It shows us how clinging to people dramatically different than ourselves can bring about unforeseen redemption. It reveals the imperative need in the world for healthy, grace-filled communities centered on mutual honor and sacrificial love. Ruth gives us all this—and much, much more. In short, through the power of the book of Ruth, we see that friendship can save the world, because Ruth and Naomi's friendship did just that. Their multiethnic, multigenerational friendship literally saved the world. And since that kind of friendship has saved our smaller, individual world more than once, we think it can save yours, too.

We are freshly aware of the stresses felt by churches anytime a church planter, pastor, or minister reaches out and asks to meet and honestly discuss the intersection of church and diversity. Usually, they call because the conflict and pain in their cities and congregations have taken a toll, and they aren't sure how to navigate the dangerous waters they find themselves in. They say something like, "We want to create an ethnically, generationally, and socioeconomically diverse church community. What can we do to build it?"

This question is more than a little challenging to answer in a one-hour lunch meeting. The pace of change in the world around us flies at a rapid, anxiety-producing speed, and the toll it takes on our relationships in the church (and outside the church) cannot be understated. What can help us? Instead of looking to blame something, anything, for our struggles—the media, our increasingly overconnected digital world, the secularization of culture at large, or that neighbor who refuses to wave when we drive by—we propose that what might help us more would be to take a moment to seek God about how to prepare ourselves and our churches for the trials of our time.

In a world full of conflicting perspectives, complex broken-ness, and confusing arguments, where can we find solid ground to build healthy lives and communities? What must we do to fulfill the call to be the faithful, overcoming people God created us to be? And how can we best love and serve the church as she weathers the storms and stresses of life to be presented "in splendor, without spot or wrinkle or anything like that, but holy and blameless" (Eph. 5:27 CSB)?

To answer these questions, we, like Ruth, need to pick up the prophetic vision to which the book points. What do we mean by *prophetic*? To find out, let's briefly hit the slopes.

MORGAN

I'm Not Getting Up

A few years ago, I fulfilled my dream of taking my kids skiing. Our family lives in Central Texas, where snow rarely falls in winter. As far as my children and I are concerned, this climate truth is a tragedy because we love winter sports of all kinds. Since the closest snowy slopes are more than a day's drive away from Austin, my children had never beheld a winter ski resort in all its frosty glory for the first ten years or so of their lives.

But this particular year, we drove north and west to Colorado, to a little mom-and-pop slope with a single lift to carry us up to the runs. It wasn't fancy, but it did the job. We stood in line to rent gear and then dropped the kids off for lessons in the basics while I scouted out the best runs for beginners, known as the "green" runs.

When I picked the kids up from ski school, they were pumped, thrilled, and fully ready to shred the mountain. I couldn't wait to help them tackle that first awkward ride on the ski lift. I didn't mind fetching the skis that flew off when they inevitably lost their balance and tumbled over. I relished picking them up, dusting them off, and encouraging them to get up and begin again.

But my then ten-year-old son, Jase, crashed one time too many and transformed into a full-blown rage machine. He lay in the snow and yelled while thrashing his arms and legs. When I skied over to him to see if he was going to be okay, he wouldn't budge.

"I'm not getting up," he announced.

"Yes, you are," I said.

"No, I'm not."

"Yes, you are."

"No, I'm not."

Finally, exasperated, I deployed some undefeatable dad logic: "Listen, buddy—that's going to be a problem. Eventually, we'll have to leave this mountain because the ski resort will close. If you don't get up, you'll be left in the snow overnight and freeze to death. You can be done, you don't have to ski anymore, but you can't stay here."

His eyes got big. Clearly, he hadn't considered his circumstances with any connection to reality whatsoever. Then these words tumbled out of the mouth of this boy, who never ceases to amaze us: "I don't want to be done," he growled. "I want to go all the way to the top and ski one of the blue runs."

For those unfamiliar with skiing, blue runs are much more challenging than the green runs. During his four-hour-long skiing career, Jase had yet to successfully ski down a single green slope from halfway up the mountain. I doubted Jase could handle the challenging blue run from the top. Plus, you know, he was seated and screaming about not moving, ever again. But I figured there was only one way to find out. I pointed at a medium-level green slope and made a deal with him. "If you can make it down *that* slope without falling, I'll take you all the way to the top."

Jase nodded, and with his jaw set in stubborn determination, we headed to the lift. For the next couple of hours, Jase failed again and again to ski down cleanly. But then, near the end of the afternoon, as the sun was beginning to set, Jase exited the lift, said nothing, pointed his skis down that mountain, and flew straight to the bottom without a single turn or swerve to slow himself.

All gas, no brakes.

I held my breath when I realized he was flying toward a group of kindergarteners congregated by the snack bar. Amazingly, Jase dug in his edges while at maximum velocity and stopped himself within two feet of destroying a group of five-year-olds. He stayed upright, turned around to look back at me, and lifted his arms to cheer in victory.

It was a glorious moment, one only surpassed by the well-earned run Jase and I took together from the top of the mountain on that blue run.

Later that night, back at our cabin, I asked Jase what motivated him to keep trying all day despite his repeated and spectacular crashes.

"I just kept thinking about going all the way to the top of the mountain with you, Dad," he said.

I just kept thinking about going all the way to the top with you, Dad.

Jase imagined going to the top of the mountain, and he imagined going there with his dad. Together, those two imagined futures catalyzed to form a vision that drew Jase beyond his current circumstances. He imagined the beauty of what it would look like beyond where he had been, thought about who he wanted to go with, and embraced every challenge necessary to achieve his vision.

In the same way, there is a stiff challenge before us of building and nurturing multiethnic, multigenerational, economically diverse churches and communities. Individually and corporately, we've face-planted in the snow of that challenge a few thousand times or more. But for those who are determined to get up this mountain, whatever the cost may be, there is a place at the top where we will raise our arms in victory, full of love for one another and in awe of the God who brought us together.

What does it take to get there?

Like a kid who chooses to get to the top of a mountain, we first need a prophetic vision. Just as Jase needed to imagine going to the top of the mountain with me, building diverse relationships and communities requires a prophetic vision of God's relational power.

We find many examples of prophetic vision throughout the Bible. For example, the Hebrew prophets consistently saw two things in their visions: something about the nature and character of God and something about their culture in need of transformation. The prophets captured something from the heart of God, talked about it, and wrote it down to call people to follow God more wholeheartedly.

New Testament prophetic ministry is a little different, although it generally shares the Hebrew prophets' end goal. New Testament prophetic ministry captures and communicates something about the heart of God for someone so they can love God more wholeheartedly. We find this spelled out in 1 Corinthians 14:3, which tells us that New Testament prophecy encourages, strengthens, and confirms what God wants to do in a life or in a certain situation.

When someone asks me how to build diverse friendships or communities, I tell them it requires making a choice, birthed out of a prophetic vision, to actively understand how and why God builds relationally with us so we can follow him more wholeheartedly.

Let's get a mountaintop look at Ruth's story for a better view of that type of prophetic vision.

Ruth the World Changer

We don't see all of this in chapter 1 of the book of Ruth, but at the end of the story, after the wedding of (spoiler alert) Boaz and Ruth, we learn that they had a son, Obed. And Obed, we read, was the father of Jesse, and Jesse had a son of his own named David, who grew up to be Israel's greatest king. Ruth, then, was David's great-grandmother, which is impressive given her backstory. But that's not the last time Ruth's name appears in the Christian scriptures.

The final mention of Ruth occurs in the opening moments of the New Testament, when the Gospel writer Matthew lists out the genealogy of Jesus. Genealogies were not an uncommon or necessarily surprising way to begin a story about a person considered in some way to be great. In the ancient world, listing someone's ancestors was a way of creating cultural worth, similar to our modern-day resume building. If someone wants to know more about us, they can speak with our references listed on our resume or job application. In the same way, Matthew is saying, *Do you want to know more about Jesus? Take a look at these people in his lineage. Their lives and stories reveal something you have to see about Jesus's identity.* Matthew went to work, and he did what we might imagine he would do: he listed King David's name—rightfully so—along with a lot of other men—some famous, some not so much—in Jesus's family line. Matthew, however, also did something remarkable and risky in his patriarchal culture: he included a handful of women in his list, including Ruth.

By mentioning Ruth, Matthew is saying, once more, *Do you want to see who Jesus is and who he came to be? Then you have to see who Ruth was. Go and read her story. When you see what Ruth did for Naomi, you will see what Jesus has done for you.*

How can the beginning of Ruth's story offer us a better view of Jesus?

As Ruth clung to Naomi, who was different from her and had nothing provisional to offer her, Jesus has clung to us. Jesus came to us as the ultimate outsider, the ultimate foreigner in our world. He doesn't come to us expecting rescue or provision, as he knows we have neither to offer on our own. Even still, Jesus looked at those totally unlike him, and his actions declared, *My people will be your people. My God will be your God. Where you go, I'll go. I'll never leave you nor forsake you.* Then Jesus did even more for us than Ruth did for Naomi when clinging to us cost him his life and last breath.

In Ruth's decision to cling to Naomi, we find a prophetic vision of *how* Jesus chooses us. We are the people Jesus chooses to cling to despite how little our lives benefit him and without regard for how unlike him we are. Jesus is divine, whereas we rely entirely on him to make us holy. Jesus saves, befriends, heals, provides for, and rescues us despite the truth that all we can offer him is our allegiance and worship. Jesus comes to us as Lord of all and Savior of the world, whereas we come as sinners wholly incapable of saving ourselves.

Once we understand that Jesus chose and loved us without regard for what he had in common with us or how he could benefit from the relationship, we can begin to do that for others. This kind of prophetic vision is what makes diverse communities possible. This vision of seeing how Ruth's choice of Naomi points to Jesus's choice of us has fueled our hearts and our local church. Preaching and teaching and reminding ourselves and our church of the beauty of this prophetic vision has helped us time and again when difficult things happen in our nation. In a diverse community, a great deal of clinging to one another is required to process cultural events and hurdles like police shootings, elections, protests, politicians' inflammatory statements, and the potentially divisive nature of media outlets. Remembering the value of the relational connection between a young Moabitess and an older Jewish woman has grounded us in the love of God for one another over and over.

With all this talk of clinging to one another and prophetic vision, we might be tempted to think that diversity for the sake of diversity alone should be our goal, but it's not and never can be. To make diversity our primary goal would be to lose our first love and forfeit our ability to fulfill Christ's command to love God with our whole heart, soul, mind, and strength as we love our neighbor as ourselves. Without something substantial and unchanging at the core of our prophetic vision, we will fall prey to the pressure to abandon it when times get tough or settle for a definition of diversity that sounds too much like the world's and not enough like God's heart. Undergirding a prophetic vision, then, is something unique that only the Christian faith gives us.

MORGAN

Theological Conviction

Years ago, while Carrie and I were campus ministers at the University of Texas, we organized an outreach for the fall semester. At that time, our campus ministry included primarily White and Black students. Campus ministries at UT in the early 2000s were largely homogenous in terms of race. While it seemed like we were more diverse than most groups, when I looked around at our group, I simultaneously felt gratitude for who was there and longing for who wasn't there—namely, students of other people groups on campus.

To live out James 2 and unite our faith with our works, we prayed and tried to act with the expectation that God would strategically add to our group. We asked God to help us reach a more diverse cross-section of the campus population. Specifically, we prayed for evangelistic open doors to Asian, Latino, and Indian students. When we ordered flyers for the outreach, we chose a stock image that happened to include a photo of students of many races. Our student group name, after all, was Every Nation Campus.

We didn't consider this a strategic choice; we simply chose a photo that included people who hadn't shown up yet. And guess what? A good number did. We longed for a campus ministry that mirrored the student population at UT. We knew God's great love extended to every student on campus, and we wanted the voices and stories shaping our community to represent as much of the student body as we could gather.

Why? Because biblical diversity begins with a theological conviction that rests upon the unique nature of the God of the universe.

As Christians, we believe that God is triune, or three in one, comprising the three persons of God the Father, God the Son, and God the Spirit. As Timothy Keller noted in his sermon, "The Triune God,"[1] we need all three uniquely diverse persons of the Trinity actively involved in our lives to form and shape us correctly. If we don't open ourselves up to the fullness of all three persons of God, we can become a little spiritually lopsided.

For example, suppose all we ever focused on was the person of God the Father. We might become too rigid, dogmatic, authoritarian, and focused on rules and boundaries and miss the grace offered through the gospel. We could become like the first-century Pharisees, consumed with right and wrong.

But if all we ever focused on was the person of the Son, while we might feel good about being forgiven and having the forever love of God in our hearts, we could get complacent without the

---

[1] Timothy Keller, "The Triune God," Redeemer Presbyterian Church, June 11, 2011, https://podcasts.apple.com/us/podcast/the-triune-god/id352660924?i =1000577424626.

compelling work of the Holy Spirit. We might not be morally legalistic, but we could get spiritually lazy.

Or if all we ever focused on was the work of the Holy Spirit—without the boundaries of a loving Father and the saving work of the Son—we might end up chasing experience endlessly for its own sake. We might not be legalistic or lazy, but we could end up missionally weak.

The diversity within the triune God produces the fullness of God's kingdom. A Father who gives boundaries, a Son who gives grace, and a Spirit who gives power work together to shape us into faithful Christ followers who are capable of loving God and loving others and who impact the world for the glory of God. Therefore, the diversity within the Trinity models the need for diversity in the church. If Trinitarian life is inherently and fundamentally diverse, why wouldn't we seek to mirror that diversity in our churches in whatever way we can? It should be no surprise that the first Christian churches were ethnically diverse. No resource existed in the world to gather every tribe and language until the sending of the Holy Spirit and the revelation of the triune nature of God.

We're grateful for the opportunity to belong to an ethnically, generationally, and socioeconomically diverse community of faith because it generally keeps us from becoming imbalanced regarding one perspective or another. However, we don't pursue ethnic, generational, or socioeconomic diversity for its own sake. We do it because a diversity of persons sits at the center of the God of the Bible, and we want to experience and express his heart as fully as we can.

Therefore, it is crucial to express that creating diverse communities isn't a growth strategy; it's a discipleship strategy. Over the years, people have accused us of prioritizing diversity as part of a self-righteous marketing strategy aimed at building a bigger church. My reply to this is simple: please try building your life/

workplace/family/church with diversity as a primary element and see for yourself if it's a good growth strategy. There is a reason there aren't that many racially diverse churches in the United States, and it isn't because churches don't want to grow. According to the National Congregations Study, which analyzed more than five thousand congregations, four out of five American congregations "remain overwhelmingly white or Black or Hispanic or Asian."[2] The study's data analyzing generational diversity in churches shows that across all religions in the United States, congregations are aging drastically, creating a majority culture above the age of sixty. Unfortunately, data regarding socioeconomic diversity within congregations in the United States is not present in this study or in any other study we have encountered. However, even if every racially diverse church was also socioeconomically and generationally diverse, modeling your church growth strategy on the success of such a small number of churches would be highly illogical. We'd like to be clear about diversity as a church growth strategy: we don't prioritize diversity to build a bigger church; we do it to cultivate faithfulness in our church and build a more robust Trinitarian vision for life and humanity.

Noticing who isn't present in our earthly communities and choosing to reach for them and cling to them isn't just a nice, feel-good idea. It's one small way to live out Jesus's holy prayer that God's kingdom would come "on earth as it is in heaven" (Matt. 6:10 NIV).

So far, we have seen that a prophetic vision opens the way to building diverse communities and that a theological conviction

---

[2] Mark Chaves, Joseph Roso, Anna Holleman, and Mary Hawkins, *Congregations in 21st Century America* (Durham, NC: Duke University, Department of Sociology, 2021), 46, https://sites.duke.edu/ncsweb/files/2022/02/NCSIV_Report_Web_FINAL2.pdf.

sustains and undergirds that vision. We need one more crucial, nonnegotiable element to bring the vision fully to life.

Relational Sacrifice

In the winter of 2021, Austin experienced a historically severe snowstorm. Our family did not snow ski that year, but we did survive one of the worst natural disasters in Texas state history. If we could leave a review for historic, unprecedented winter storms, we would leave zero stars. Snow and ice made the roads impassable, the temperature dropped far below freezing for days, millions of Texans lost power, and more than two hundred people died.

On the second morning of the storm, the roads were still somewhat navigable, so I drove slowly to the only open grocery store nearby. Our non-four-wheel-drive SUV barely made it there. Carrie white-knuckled the passenger door and prayed quietly under her breath while I steered us through the ice and snow. There was little food left to purchase in the store, but as we handed the necessities we could find to the cashier, Carrie thanked her for coming to work.

"My boyfriend has a four-wheel drive. Otherwise, I wouldn't even be here," the cashier said. "We only had two people working here yesterday, and all the other grocery stores closed. We had to lock the doors early because there weren't enough cashiers to ring up all the orders before closing."

After our precarious drive home, we received reports of the problems worsening in Austin. The Texas power grid had failed. Power went out across the state, but Austin was hit particularly hard. The storm, we were learning, had caused many of our church members to be without power and water for days. Carrie and I huddled under blankets in our own home, tended dripping faucets to avoid pipes bursting, prepared our kids for the next power outage, and acknowledged that we were living in the middle of a humanitarian crisis.

Working together, our church staff of about twenty-five set up a call-in system to match people in need of help with people capable of offering help. Many people were trapped in their homes. They were shivering in the dark, melting snow to flush toilets, and eating dinner by flashlight. Some of our friends lost everything when their frozen pipes burst. Others were burning their furniture to stay warm. We used four-wheel-drive vehicles to pick up folks who had been freezing in the dark for days. It wasn't hard to find people needing help during that time because almost everyone needed help.

I rode into Central Austin with one of our members, a White man from Kentucky who drove a big pickup truck. We went to move three young Black women whose apartment had lost water and power into a friend's house. Along the way, we towed a police car out of one ditch, pushed another vehicle out of another ditch, and found shelter for a homeless man. In the middle of all that, once those women were safely in the warm truck, one of them said, "I'll never look at a White man in a pickup truck the same way again!" And then we all laughed because, really, how had this become our lives?

Carrie stayed at our house to make sure our own pipes didn't freeze and burst as we awaited the next round of ice and snow. I moved into the church building with a few other staff members because, at the city's request, our church became a 24/7 shelter facility. We were one of seven churches in the Austin area that the city of Austin used to house displaced people until they could figure out their next steps. When we decided to do this, our building had managed to retain power and water. But at the literal hour we started receiving people, our water lines froze, and we were reduced to one working, flushable toilet (if we poured water in the tank ourselves). One working, flushable toilet in a building for thirty-five people isn't ideal, but it was better than flooded apartments and homes without heat. To keep that toilet flushing, we scraped the ice off the parking lot throughout the day, carried it inside in big trash barrels, and melted it in pots on the stove to keep our toilet going.

While this happened at the church, the Mosaic street ministry team checked on our homeless friends. We knew we needed a miracle to provide for them or they would die in the storm. One of our street ministry leaders got on the phone and raised approximately sixty thousand dollars to feed and house two hundred homeless people in hotels during the storm. Unfortunately, that fantastic solution only lasted one night for some of them because, the next day, the hotels lost their electricity and sent them out to sleep on the streets again. Complicating things, the weather forecast predicted a temperature of two degrees Fahrenheit.

Unwilling to abandon anyone to the elements, we moved those displaced homeless people into our facility. Shortly thereafter, the police began bringing patients from a psychiatric hospital that had lost power and water to stay in our church. The hospital had lost utilities, and had turned its patients out on the street. The police picked up those who didn't have family or friends to stay with and brought them to us.

We ended up with approximately seventy people living in our church for almost a week, with one working toilet, in the middle of a pandemic with COVID-19 cases at an all-time high, long before vaccines were available to the public. We couldn't melt the snow fast enough to keep the toilet flushing, so we called the city manager, who had promised to provide anything we might need. We asked for two portable toilets, but the city told us they were, unfortunately, out.

That day, for the first time in my life, I prayed for something I had never prayed for before. I gathered our pastoral team on a Zoom call, and we all pleaded with the Holy Spirit to send us some portable toilets. Within five minutes after our impromptu prayer meeting, the city manager somehow miraculously found the last two portable toilets in the city. When he called me, I said, "Bring 'em over!" And they did.

Toilets were progress, but the situation worsened by the hour inside the building. Some of our guests were so scared and confused after being taken from the psychiatric hospital that they began to urinate on themselves and on our floor. Fights between some of our homeless guests broke out as their anxiety rose. Our shelter was being run by volunteers, not professionals, and some began to fear for their safety.

We were in a difficult situation. We were housing people who were unpredictable, under great stress, and volatile, but they would not survive the night if they weren't inside our building. We called the police and asked for an officer who could stay on the premises during the night to keep everyone safe. Unfortunately, given that the city was in a state of emergency, all available officers were already assigned across the city.

Our pastoral team prayed again, not for toilets, but for a police officer. We reminded God how much he loved the people staying in our church. We begged again, and it worked again. Minutes later, my phone rang. It was the commander of the Austin Police Department. He heard we needed their help. What could he do for us?

An officer arrived just in time to make our parking lot his base for the night, alleviating our volunteers' justifiable concerns and ensuring our safety for at least one more night.

In the following days, our church members began to give and serve spontaneously and sacrificially. When other churches heard about the shoestring operation we had organized, they sent us money to help anyone in dire need. By God's grace, we raised so much money we were able to pay for hotels and food for weeks for many of our guests who had lost everything and then pay for apartments and homes full of new furniture to replace what they had lost.

All of this was life-changing to live through and witness, but it's important to note that while nearly all the citizens of our city suffered, not all of us suffered equally. Some parts of the city retained power throughout the storm, and some went days without power and water in homes that weren't designed to tolerate subfreezing temperatures. The city's wealthier areas maintained almost uninterrupted power and water access during the storm because they shared power circuits with critical facilities, like hospitals. Meanwhile, poorer neighborhoods, which don't generally share real estate with critical facilities, lost their utilities first and had them restored last. While I don't envy anyone the task of making difficult organizational decisions in the middle of a catastrophic storm, what happened in Austin during that storm seemed incredibly unjust. In Austin, as in many cities, most residents of those more impoverished areas are Black and Latino people. In other words, on average, poor communities of color suffered most during that winter storm. Why is this detail important to note?

The poor and homeless were not in the rooms when the city's electrical infrastructure was organized long before that storm hit. They weren't physically present when electrical outages were being monitored during the storm. Historically, poorer neighborhoods have suffered more acutely in natural disasters because they lack the resources wealthier residents rely on to overcome the problems caused by disasters. Unless the most vulnerable are figuratively carried into the room where leaders make decisions about how to best protect and provide for a city, they can easily be underserved and overlooked. The work required to undergird a population in the middle of a catastrophe begins long before the catastrophe hits. The winter storm that hit Austin in February 2021 would not have caused as much suffering or as many deaths had the city, state, and utility companies built a system that ensured rolling blackouts could have successfully left people without electricity for no more than an hour or two at a time.

When we realized how many people in Austin faced days without electricity or water while temperatures plummeted well below freezing, Mosaic leaned into the relational grid we had built in the city before the storm hit. We reached out to anyone we had previously met and connected with to help ensure anyone in need received the care and supplies they needed. We told everyone we had clung to within Mosaic and outside our congregation to call us when they needed something. We also invited them all to offer any help they might be able to provide. Our decision to love and care for those in need in Austin long before that catastrophic storm hit meant we were already connected to the people and places that would feel the effects of the storm first, as well as people and organizations capable of providing aid.

In any gathering or community, if we don't notice who isn't present when we gather, who has been left vulnerable and disconnected, we might never see who isn't safe or cared for in our broader community. And if we don't notice who has been overlooked or marginalized outside our gathering, we will never find ways to reach or serve them as Christ has commanded us to do. You can't cling to someone if you don't know them. You can't go all the way up the mountain with someone if you haven't skied the easier runs with them first.

Ruth had known Naomi for many years before she clung to her and made a covenant to go all the way to Bethlehem with her.

Her decision to cling to Naomi required deep love and relational sacrifice, and it resulted in making her part of God's greatest story ever as a woman counted in the family line of Jesus. Her choice to cling to Naomi also reveals how earnestly God honors those who will cling to others as he has clung to us.

All we want, in the end, is to form the kind of friendships that will take us all the way to the top of the mountain, where we can raise our arms and cheer for all God has done in our midst. Before we start our hike up, though, let's drop down into Ruth's story.

STORIES
from our FRIENDS
A Hope for Beloved Community

BY TERRANCE L. GREEN, PHD

In her powerful book, *Killing Rage: Ending Racism*, scholar and cultural critic bell hooks writes about the necessity of each person claiming their unique identity and cultural legacy to form a beloved community. Here, hooks beautifully describes how our lives can be a mosaic—despite our differences.[3]

A mosaic is one of the most beautiful and ancient forms of art. Its beauty is found in bringing together a diversity of pieces that maintain their separate uniqueness yet form a splendid collective.

However, creating a mosaic is difficult.

It's even more difficult to create a mosaic of people within the church context in the United States because our lives are separated and shaped by anti-Black racism and violence, White supremacy, patriarchy, and a host of other sinful and oppressive forces.

To be honest, as a Black man living in the United States, I still struggle at times with believing in a church mosaic.

While I am glad to be a member of Mosaic Church Austin, there have been many times when people did not "get it," mainly White folks. For example, during my first men's retreat, a White man—whom I had never met—interrupted my conversation with another Black person and boisterously

---

[3] bell hooks, *Killing Rage: Ending Racism* (New York: Henry Holt, 1995).

started yelling at me about how demonic and anti-White public schools are.

There have also been several times when White people have mistaken me for other Black men who attend the church. Additionally, I have had many conversations with White people at the church about race and racism that went wrong quickly, and to be honest, some conversations ended relationships.

I could go on.

Yet, despite these and other incidents, I remain hopeful.

I remain hopeful because of the racial, ethnic, culturally diverse, and beautiful mosaic God has worked through some of the community groups that my family and I have been part of. These groups have been a true source of joy, strength, and friendship.

I remain hopeful because of the church's leadership—Morgan, Carrie, and the elders—who are steadfast in being a multiethnic, multigenerational church. Their resolve has cost them close friends and church members, has led to them being misunderstood and talked about, and much more. Yet they continue to persevere.

I remain hopeful because Mosaic has created space to name, grieve, and act against racial injustice and other forms of injustice.

I remain hopeful because the church realizes that diversity alone is not enough to realize God's justice.

I remain hopeful (and grateful) because of the opportunities to exhort and share God's Word on Sunday mornings. Through these opportunities, I remain in awe when people who are of a different race, political leaning, and lived experience tell me how God used me to touch their lives.

I remain hopeful because the church continues to pray, struggle, lament, celebrate, and live out what it means to truly be a mosaic and a beloved community.

Chapter 2

A POWERFUL CHOICE

The Covenant of Clinging

In the days when the judges ruled, there was a famine in the land. So a man from Bethlehem in Judah, together with his wife and two sons, went to live for a while in the country of Moab.

—Ruth 1:1 NIV

Ruth's story begins in roughly 1300 BC by introducing us to a man named Elimelech and his family, who lived in the Jewish town of Bethlehem.

Names, as always, are important in Bible stories, and Elimelech, which means "my God is King," and his wife Naomi, which means "pleasant," were people with names whose fortunes free-fell in life with tragic poetic irony. When a massive famine hit the nation of Israel and Bethlehem, Naomi and Elimelech fled in desperation as refugees to the hostile neighboring nation of Moab to try to survive and carve out a new life. Although they fled tragic circumstances, tragedy still found them in Moab, where Elimelech and Naomi would eventually live out the opposite of the meanings of their names.

Between the lines of the biblical narrative, we find evidence that Elimelech's suffering caused him to abandon his faith. He gave his two sons the pagan, Moabite names of Mahlon ("sick") and Chilion ("wasting away"). It also seems likely that Elimelech failed to teach his sons to fear God, as they grew up and married non-Jewish, idol-worshiping women, which was forbidden by Jewish law. But isn't this how it goes in life, sometimes? We begin as "my God is King," only to face a series of blows that weaken our faith to the darkness surrounding us. Can you imagine emigrating, leaving everyone you've ever known, staving off starvation, facing racial and cultural hostility, and having little to nothing to support your family and faith? Poor Elimelech. That's a heavy haul for anyone.

But then, things didn't just go from bad to worse for this little family; they moved from worse to impossible. The women in Elimelech's family (Naomi and her two Moabite daughters-in-law, Ruth and Orpah) were forced into their own private "no man's land" when all three men in their family died. First Elimelech died, followed by Mahlon and Chilion ten years later. Ruth, Orpah, and Naomi became stranded in a male-dominated culture, without children, without options, without provision, and most of all, without hope.

What would they do? Where could they go? In the middle of her grief, Naomi, the matriarch, decided to journey back to Israel because Bethlehem ("house of bread") was rumored to finally have food back on the shelves. At first, Ruth and Orpah set out on the road back to Bethlehem with Naomi for the seven- to ten-day walk over exposed, rugged terrain.

At this point, we should pause a bit and acknowledge that many of us are walking through "on the road" moments like Naomi, Orpah, and Ruth in Ruth 1. All kinds of national tragedies and cultural or societal famine-like losses have struck the world recently.

Along with our personal and individual losses, we've faced, collectively, a viral pandemic, a major economic downturn, constant political conflict and upheaval, historic inflation, and racial injustice, to name a few. These trials have caused disruption in our personal lives, families and churches, and cities and nation. Some of us have relocated, as Elimelech and Naomi did. We have been cut off from our old lives and relationships, which frayed and damaged our mental and physical well-being. Possibly, some of us have lost someone we loved in the middle of our struggle and at the height of our pain.

When the weight of sorrow and loss upends our plans and relationships, as happened with Ruth, Orpah, and Naomi, the question naturally arises: Where do we go next? How do we find the strength to carry our losses as we move forward?

In many ways, life is a continual journey on the road to a foreign-seeming future. Like Elimelech and Naomi on their way to Moab, we seek a safe refuge. Like Naomi and Ruth, we long to return home and be restored. But are we on a road that leads to the right place? What do we need to sustain us on our way? Is the home and safety we dream of possible to attain?

When Naomi paused to consider these kinds of questions on the road, she turned to her daughters-in-law and urged them not to follow her to Israel. She said:

> "Each of you go back to your mother's home. May the Lord show kindness to you as you have shown to the dead and to me. May the Lord grant each of you rest in the house of a new husband." She kissed them, and they wept loudly. (Ruth 1:8–9 CSB)

Naomi proved her commitment to pragmatism here. She grasped the difficulty in the journey ahead, as well as the challenges Ruth and Orpah would encounter as widows, foreigners, and racial and religious outsiders should they arrive safely at their destination. She said, *Friends, the odds aren't in your favor in Bethlehem. Go back.*

At first, both Orpah and Ruth brushed off Naomi. They refused to leave her. They thanked her for the heads-up, allowed that life would be tough, but insisted on staying with Naomi. Somehow, their refusal did not convince Naomi to let them travel with her. Perhaps Naomi picked up on a lack of certainty in Orpah's voice. Perhaps she wondered if their manners overrode their common sense. Naomi didn't let up. She urged them more forcefully a second time. She painted a detailed picture of their possible future in Israel, including the kicker of the unlikeliness of finding husbands as Moabites in a Jewish town. With a bit of dark humor, Naomi explained their best shot at remarrying would require a ridiculous scenario: Naomi would have to find a husband, begin miraculously ovulating again, and birth sons for them to marry. But even if such a fairy tale were possible, would they want to wait around for their new husbands to grow up? Of course not, she insisted. *That would be kind of weird, you know.*

Then Naomi revealed her deepest pain: "the LORD's hand has turned against me" (Ruth 1:13 NIV)! Naomi couldn't imagine who, in their right mind, would want to be connected to someone cursed with so many brutally bitter circumstances. She couldn't imagine how Ruth would respond by making a powerful choice that would fill both their lives in unexpected ways.

We wish we could say we've never experienced a time in our lives similar to Naomi's moment here on the road. However, even in our darkest times, the light of Ruth's powerful choice has lit the way for us. Let's look at one such time.

MORGAN

On the Road to Together

Years ago, I began in campus ministry at the University of Texas with an already-established group of students. I relocated from working in campus ministry at my alma mater, the University of Houston, to replace a UT ministry team that had moved to pioneer a new campus ministry in California.

Leadership transitions are never easy, and this one followed the pack in that regard. Some leftover dysfunction and active sabotage aimed at me by the remaining students made my job extra fun. Many of those students repented later for their poor choices, but for a while, we struggled to connect as a group. Deep frustration arose in my heart because all my efforts to lead well backfired. Our Bible studies were poorly attended, my boss didn't support or believe in me, and I was mostly financially broke. The pleasantness of my ministry calling emptied out, and the bitterness of real life set in.

In a discouraging start to my fall semester as the group leader, only fifteen students showed up for our first campus ministry meeting. We hobbled along with a ragtag group of students who missed their old campus ministers. I was the outsider in many ways, and bearing the weight of that reality prepared my heart for what the road ahead held for all of us.

A few months into that school year, three women's basketball players walked into Bible study one night. They had been invited by a friend of a friend and were the only Black people in a fairly homogenous room full of White people. Being an "only" in a new environment is challenging, and I could tell that these young athletes felt the full weight of the divide between them and the other students present. An unexpected prayer for anyone who might feel like an outsider bubbled up in my heart: *Lord, make this the kind of place where everyone can see someone like them when they walk in.*

My heart began to beat for a true expression of ethnic diversity in our group; I desired to help create a space where anyone could belong. Just as Naomi's experience as a foreign refugee created an awareness of what Ruth and Orpah potentially faced in Bethlehem, my challenges of being the outsider heightened my hope that others wouldn't face the same difficulty. Like Naomi on the road to Bethlehem, I didn't know who (if anyone) would join me on the journey. Nor did I know how this moment would shape me for all that lay ahead. I simply knew God had asked me to create a new kind of space as a leader. Before I share what happened next in that fateful semester, let's return to Naomi, Orpah, and Ruth and examine their choices to better understand the women who made them.

Ruth's Choice to Cling

When given a choice between a familiar, easier life with people just like her or life among people of a different race and culture, Orpah turned back, but Ruth did not. Ruth 1:14–15 (CSB) says, "Again they wept loudly, and Orpah kissed her mother-in-law, but Ruth clung to her. Naomi said, 'Look, your sister-in-law has gone back to her people and to her gods. Follow your sister-in-law.'" Sometimes Orpah is criticized for her choice to go back. Certainly, since we know how Ruth's choice ended, it's easy to judge Orpah's choice as shortsighted. Just as we regret not buying real estate in downtown Austin in 2003 (we would be millionaires three times over by now), it's possible Orpah regretted leaving Naomi at some point in her future. However, the writer of Ruth graciously acknowledges the difficulty and inner turmoil Orpah faced and doesn't judge her for it. Orpah counted the potential cost of staying with Naomi and chose to kiss her mother-in-law goodbye. Interestingly, Jewish tradition teaches that Orpah turned back at the four-mile mark on their journey.[1] According to legend, these four miles are evidence that Orpah became the mother of Goliath and his three brothers. Orpah received one giant son per mile as her penance, apparently. Although fascinating and a little humorous, this legend isn't supported by any historic writings or the biblical timeline.

We hope Orpah's road home led to redemption and restoration of some kind. However, she's never heard from again in the Bible. Her name did pop up roughly three thousand years after she lived, though, when one American mother, naming her daughter, unintentionally misspelled Orpah, switching the "p" and the "r." That baby girl grew up to be one of the world's most powerful people. But that's another story altogether.

Thankfully, the Bible shares exactly how things went for Ruth when she chose to cling to this multiethnic, multigenerational friendship. Initially, the path she and Naomi endured wasn't so great. After the losses of her father-in-law, her husband, and her brother-in-law, Ruth endured yet another loss: the loss of her sister-in-law, Orpah, who was the only other person in Ruth's family who fully knew Ruth and her culture. Orpah had been in Ruth's life for more than ten years, but when the path became too arduous, Orpah simply walked. And when she walked, Naomi pressed Ruth one more time to go back.

When given the final chance to go back home to her own gods, her own people, and her own culture, Ruth made what is arguably the single most powerful choice in all the Old Testament. Ruth chose the path that values multigenerational, multiethnic relationships over a familiar and comfortable life, and she covenanted to remain with Naomi all the way to the end:

---

[1] Barry Dov Walfish, "The Defamation of Orpah," *TheTorah.com*, accessed August 31, 2022, https://www.thetorah.com/article/the-defamation-of-orpah.

> But Ruth replied: "Don't plead with me to abandon you
> or to return and not follow you. For wherever you go,
> I will go, and wherever you live, I will live; your people
> will be my people, and your God will be my God.
> Where you die, I will die, and there I will be buried. May
> the LORD punish me, and do so severely, if anything but
> death separates you and me." (Ruth 1:16–17 CSB)

In this beautiful vow of relational fidelity, Ruth not only committed to her mother-in-law, but she also proved that she converted to faith in the one true God, away from the false gods of the Moabites. She called God by the Hebrew name *Yahweh*, which is his special, covenantal name in the Hebrew scriptures. This was not the choice of an emotional woman who just sort of liked her mother-in-law an awful lot. Ruth's powerful choice was not motivated by feelings, which can shift and change with our circumstances. Choices based on feelings alone don't result in redemptive futures.

At the bottom of choices that move heaven and earth are not feelings, but an allegiance to relational connection above all else. Undergirding strong relationships between spouses, friends, parents and children, siblings, or the people in strong neighborhoods, vibrant churches, and other communities is not all the feelings we have in common, but the choice to do the hard work necessary to protect and retain our connection to one another based upon God's covenantal love toward us—even when we don't necessarily feel like doing that hard work.

Ruth made a covenant relationship with Naomi when she declared they would walk together no matter what, and she promised that the only thing that could separate them was death itself. Those were big, powerful, and sort of scary words when you consider their weightiness. However, those are the kind of covenant words that move God's kingdom forward. Especially in generationally, ethnically, and socioeconomically diverse relationships and friendships, those are the kind of words God uses to complete his greatest work.

Where could Ruth have possibly heard of a covenant like this before? Perhaps, and most likely, Ruth had learned about God's covenant from Naomi. Perhaps Naomi had told her about Abraham and the way God passed between the pieces to make a covenant with him. Perhaps Naomi had told her about Moses and the covenant God made when he promised his forever fidelity to a nation of former slaves.

Somehow, Ruth understood God's covenantal love well enough to choose to covenant with Naomi. This powerful choice we make toward one another, based upon God's covenant love toward us, is what creates and sustains the power for friendships of all kinds. Ruth (likely) learned it from Naomi, and Carrie and I have caught glimpses of it from having friends of different backgrounds and perspectives. Many of those friendships can be traced back to my first semester as a campus minister when God flipped my bitter circumstances upside down.

MORGAN

A Miraculous Turn

Back to my pivotal first semester as a campus minister. Not long after those first basketball players showed up at Bible study, my friend and fellow campus minister, Andrea, and I began discussing how to create diverse Christian communities on campus. Andrea worked specifically with student athletes, and she invited me to speak at her women's Bible study one night. I was the only male in the room, as well as the only White person. I shared my heart to see God bring people of all backgrounds together. I shared that achieving this dream would require us to show up ready to love people unlike us, and then I invited them to a big campus out-reach event our ministry had planned in a few weeks. Andrea and I asked them if they had any friends who might want to come hear the gospel.

As it turned out, they did.

A few weeks later, at that outreach, the unforeseen and mirac-ulous happened. Black student after Black student began to come and give their lives to Christ. In the following weeks, we witnessed a small revival in the Black community at UT. After that week was over, the conversions didn't stop and continued over the next month or so. In total, approximately fifty Black students came to faith that semester. Until that time, our group had topped out at about fifteen to twenty students.

Suddenly, at the age of twenty-five, along with two other White leaders, I experienced the joy and challenge of leading a predominantly Black student ministry at a university that refused to enroll any Black students for the first seventy-three years it existed. As it turned out, we were all in for the adventure of a life-time. Our campus ministry grew and grew as the years passed, and we became more diverse as we went on (more on that later in the book). One year, we were even nominated as the "Black Student Group of the Year" at UT, which delighted (and amused) us, given how many of our students weren't Black.

All of this began in 2001, at a time when discussions about how walking a path of interracial friendships and pursuing racial justice in a ministry context were nearly nonexistent. The other White campus ministers and I didn't have books about diverse faith communities to offer us help. We were foreigners in the land of diversity much the same way Ruth became a foreigner in Bethlehem. We were people who wanted to love and serve our community, so we did what leaders must do when they're in over their heads. We showed up. We listened. We apologized when we made mistakes. We schooled ourselves on what our students loved. We did all the things we knew to do to love people well: we met their families when they came to visit, we prayed with them when they were sick or injured, we listened to their favorite music and watched their favorite movies, we prayed for them when they took exams, and we preached faith and hope and trust and love in God to them every chance we got.

The thing about loving people who are different from you is that once the relationship is established, the effort and acts of love required to sustain a diverse friendship aren't much different than those required with friends who are just like you. That fruitful outreach became a turning point in our lives, just as Naomi's "go back" speech was a turning point in the story for both Ruth and Orpah. We had to choose whether to cling to people radically different from us or "go back" to "worshiping our own 'gods'"—that is, worshiping God in a culturally familiar way with people just like us. We chose to celebrate our differences, share our truest selves, laugh at ourselves when we often bobbled things, and thank God for a chance to see him do something only he could do: bridge the unbridgeable gaps.

God took my little prayer from that first fall semester meeting and faithfully grew its fruit into what is now at the core of Mosaic Church in Austin, Texas. I'm grateful so many people were willing to say yes to the opportunity to plunge headfirst into God's love for all people. Like Ruth and Naomi, we still had a long way to go as we worked to love one another through all the storms we would face, but the imperative first choice to cling had been made.

Many times since those early days of campus ministry, people have asked us, *How can we love and be in community with people different from us? It's too difficult. It's too messy. They* [fill in the blank here with another people group] *always do this, don't get that, and certainly don't understand what it's like to be us.*

47

Our answer is a consistent, simple, loving, but challenging question: Do you want to be a Ruth or an Orpah? Do you want to close the gap with people different from you based on God's covenant love toward you, or do you want to walk away and return somewhere with less conflict, misunderstanding, and negative cultural history?

Or, to put it more simply, what are you willing to risk so you won't miss out on the good stuff?

Don't Pass on the Good Stuff

When I imagine Ruth, Naomi, and Orpah on the fateful road to Bethlehem, I see three women who have been through a great deal of loss, love, and life together. They remind me of the students God added to our ministry in the early aughts. They remind me of our family hunkered down in the middle of 2020. They remind me of the church community we hold dear today. And they remind me of the little church Carrie and I attended when we were still students in college.

The church met in a converted crack house in the Third Ward of Houston, Texas. The only ventilation available on hot Houston days was the minimal breeze blowing in through open windows and old bullet holes in the walls from days gone by. We spent many Sundays in that little house, singing gospel songs to gospel tracks played from a silver boom box. Despite often being the only White people sitting in the rows of folding chairs, that church family was part of where we learned how friendship and belonging can do transformative and redemptive miracles.

One weeknight, we gathered with a group of people from church to hang out and play games. We expected cards and dominoes, but we were instead introduced to an interactive game called "pass the rap." In this game, everyone sat in a circle and began a collective beat. One person then began creating an improvisational poem, also known as freestyle rapping, and after finishing his or her verse, the person would "pass" the rap to another person in the group.

Always, Carrie and I enjoyed the vocal stylings presented by our friends. And always, we dreaded being passed the rap. Because always, our raps were lame and fell flat.

But even when I said something along the lines of "My name is Morgan and I'm here to say that I love Jesus in a major way," clearly deserving to be schooled and humbled for the pitiful attempt, my friends would cheer. They laughed and insisted I was improving. They passed me the rap again, possibly just for the fun of discovering whether I could think of two English words that rhymed other than *say* and *way* (the answer, predictably, was no).

When I imagine Ruth, Orpah, and Naomi on that road to Bethlehem, I imagine them passing the rap, in a way. I see Ruth and Orpah clapping and swaying as Naomi holds her hands to her mouth to beatbox for them. I hear Naomi lay down some heartfelt lines about how desperate her situation is. She insists by rhyme they shouldn't have to share in her misery. I continue listening as she finishes by telling them to go back where there's more hope, and then she passes the rap to them. Orpah pauses, considers picking it up, but instead kisses her mother-in-law farewell and lets the rap pass to Ruth. Ruth picks up right where Naomi's rap ended, and her rhythm and poetry response becomes a full and complete mic-drop moment. Game over. Ruth's words win.

From then on, with those words, Naomi's people would be Ruth's people. Naomi's God would be Ruth's God. Even if others saw Ruth as an outsider, she would never allow herself to be separated from her mother-in-law. In a world that offered Naomi anything but a just and loving set of circumstances, Ruth chose to try to even the scales by laying her life down to love her mother-in-law.

Unity, belonging, and diverse friendships are not flowers that grow and bloom haphazardly without any effort or sacrifice. Instead, when our intentional choice to cling to one another stems from God's covenantal love as Ruth's did, a better future awaits us despite the storm battering us today. But we can only get there together.

STORIES from our FRIENDS

The Value of Honest Friendships

BY KH

Honestly, I think Laura and I would've been friends if we had met at a park, school, or any of the kids' play spaces that Austin holds. We both chat people up, and our girls are the same age, so it would've been natural. But I don't think we would've had the level of depth and transparency that our friendship has had pretty much from the beginning if it wasn't framed in the diverse church setting that Mosaic provided. Laura was raised in Oklahoma, and I was raised in New York City. I'm a Black woman, and Laura is a White and Mexican woman. So yes, you can assume that we were raised differently and with different viewpoints or acquired certain ones along the way.

When we spoke about sharing our story for this book, one of the things that Laura said is that if you surround yourself with people that are an echo chamber, you are going to hear exactly what you want to hear. The issue with staying in your comfort zone is it's not a place where you're challenged and can grow. We started a community group together with one other family, and it was clear from the beginning that things would get "real." This picked up with the death of Trayvon Martin.

In the mid-2010s, the increased coverage of police violence in the United States led to some gut-wrenching conversations.

Our church started a series of meetings called "The Gospel And . . ." that explored diversity in all aspects. Although these large group meetings were vital, it was in the small moments in our homes that we felt safe to share in a less filtered way.

One day, I told a story about driving my husband to work. That day, I wore a pair of old leggings and hadn't done my hair for the day. We were in a rush, and I thought to myself, "Crap, I hope I don't get pulled over." Because in those critical moments, every single additional thing about how you present yourself could be the difference between you going about your day or it taking a drastic turn. Laura saw the fear that rushes over me every time I drive a car. And she realized that she never has to think like that. That's when she said she *felt it*. She could feel the pain and fear, which created a level of empathy that she had not felt before. And that has allowed her to have conversations with people that I may never have had.

Even though there is much physical distance between us now, our transparent conversations continue to this day. As the divide between people seems to get bigger, I am reminded of the vulnerability, the grace, the ability to say hard things to each other, and how good that can be. This is the reason that I look for a diverse church in whatever city I live in. This is the reason that I look for a church that is willing to have these conversations. It has made my life richer and deeper in love than almost anything else I could've ever imagined.

Chapter 3

PRINCIPLED CHOICES

Five Important Truths

So the two women went on until they came to Bethlehem. When they arrived in Bethlehem, the whole town was stirred because of them, and the women exclaimed, "Can this be Naomi?"

—Ruth 1:19 NIV

Ruth's powerful choice to cling to Naomi was tested the moment she and Naomi arrived back in Bethlehem. After their weeklong trek, Ruth and Naomi's appearance created a stir in town as a crowd of old friends gathered to hear Naomi spill the tea about her tale. When we consider the slower pace of ancient life, it's not hard to imagine the thrill of Naomi's return to the people of Bethlehem. There was no mail service between Moab and Bethlehem. Naomi hadn't posted photos on social media to show all her old friends her digs in Moab. She hadn't sent e-vites to them for her husband's funeral. Naomi had lived through tragedy after tragedy without the details making their back to Bethlehem. Now that she stood before them, in the flesh, they wanted the scoop.

In response to their requests for details, Naomi changed her name to highlight the most crucial plot point, and she then offered a shockingly short explanation of her life story.

> Don't call me Naomi; call me Bitter. The Strong One has dealt me a bitter blow. I left here full of life, and GOD has brought me back with nothing but the clothes on my back. Why would you call me Naomi? God certainly doesn't. The Strong One ruined me. (Ruth 1:20–21 *The Message*)

CARRIE

If I were Ruth at this moment, it's safe to say a fairly strong response would have arisen in my heart. I would have thought something like, *Nothing on your back? What about that speech I just gave about being with you, your God, and your people until I die? Now you have—how did you put it—*nothing *but the clothes on your back? Hello! Naomi! I am literally standing right next to you.*

Naomi's heartbreaking claim that she had returned with absolutely nothing proves that when we're in pain and hurting, we often can't see the best thing right in front of our noses. Ruth, though potentially offended by Naomi's blindness, didn't take the bait of offense and take her ball and go home to Moab. She didn't just cling on a dusty road in the middle of nowhere; she clung when her mother-in-law called her nothing.

It's important to note that the relational grit Ruth displayed relied not only on her ability to cling to Naomi as a person, Naomi's people as a community, and Naomi's God as her God, but to the overarching principles that linked Ruth to Naomi, the Jewish people, and the one true God. When trials and storms arise, our ability to remain connected to the principles of faith, trust, and love are essential to the survival of our relationships.

Mosaic is a church full of diverse people, and therefore, it is a community rife with conflicts. If I were to list the many disputes we've faced as a church in the 2020s alone, there are more than could fit on these pages. As we've continually faced challenging, complicated choices about the future, our friend and fellow church elder, John, consistently says, "We make the right choice, at the right time, for the right reason." John's words are a good reminder that when we know our choices will shape us for an unpredictable future, we must stand on principles we know to be true, no matter what lies ahead.

Let's take a deeper look at what we are calling "action principles" that can help us make the right choice, at the right time, for the right reason, as Ruth did, and cling to one another, no matter the offense or difficulty we may face.

MORGAN

Action Principle 1:
Be Prepared for Satan's Dirty Tricks

As we discuss friendships in this book, we stand on the foundational reality that God created humans with a deep need for connection and community. After God created Adam in Genesis 2 and put him in the garden, God famously said it wasn't good for Adam to be alone. The first "need" the first person ever experienced was relational in nature, and so God created Eve to meet that need. God's interpersonal directive for humanity since then has run along these lines: *Go and love one another as I love you.* If only achieving God's agenda came more easily for us all!

It should not surprise us that when Satan came to try to wreck God's world the first time, he went straight to the person God created to meet Adam's need for a relationship. Unfortunately, because his strategy was so effective, Satan has been copying and pasting this viral attack aimed at separating people ever since. We have a real spiritual enemy. The first principle that protects our relationships is simply this: God and our enemy, Satan, have different agendas for our relationships. God longs for connection; Satan desires separation.

In Naomi's bitter Bethlehem homecoming, the enemy threw a hardcore relational strain at Ruth. God had an agenda to advance redemptive history by bringing and keeping Ruth and Naomi together. Satan took his best shot at breaking it all up when Naomi declared her emptiness—at the exact moment Ruth stood beside her, full of promises. How would they bridge this difference in perspective, along with their different ethnicities, religious backgrounds, and ages? Who was right? What was true?

Soon after I came to faith in college, I moved into one half of a two-bedroom, one-bath duplex with a couple of other guys. Like every other decision made at age nineteen, it seemed like a good idea at the time. For the fall semester, things went swimmingly. My roommates were my friend Matt, who was raising his support to become a full-time campus minister, and my baseball teammate Chris. Matt and Chris shared the slightly bigger bedroom, while I had the smaller room to myself. That fall semester involved some of the best times in my college life. We three lived like kings, watching college football on Saturdays together and eating every night as only men in their twenties can.

I finished up finals and headed home for Christmas break. One month later, I returned to find two additional roommates living with us. Matt had, without a word, moved all my belongings into his and Chris's old room, which I suddenly shared with two strangers. Matt and Chris moved over to my room. As a bonus to the newly cramped quarters, somehow, my rent had increased despite my space decreasing. I would love to try to explain how this was possible, but like most moments of relational strain, it was complicated.

I was beyond offended. I couldn't look Matt in the eye. I internally fumed and churned until I could barely pray or read my Bible. My bitterness was killing me. What was just? What was fair? Who was right? Who was wrong?

I thought I knew, but I didn't have a clue.

One night, as I biked across campus in the dark on my way home from baseball practice, I prayed, "Help me, God. I need the grace to forgive."

Suddenly, I felt the Holy Spirit's presence right there with me on my five-speed. I inexplicably heard the Holy Spirit ask me a question, straight out of Isaiah 6. It was a question I didn't see coming: *Who will go for me?*

Somehow, I knew those words meant God was calling me into vocational ministry. Then I heard the next question from Isaiah's call: *Whom shall I send?* As tears ran down my face, I answered aloud, in the dark, pedaling furiously: *I will go. Send me.*

I had come to God for help with my relational offense, but God decided to address a more significant part of his redemptive will in my life. In a moment that miraculously arose out of nowhere and lasted forever, God freed me to answer his call, and he also freed me from the bitterness I felt toward my roommates.

Matt and I had a long talk when I returned to the duplex. In the middle of a misunderstanding, a more profound friendship established itself. Matt and I eventually became lifelong friends and campus ministry partners. Years later, he and his wife, Christy, planted an incredible church in Marseille, France. They have seen countless French and Muslim people redeemed by the love of Jesus. Matt is a better and braver man than I am, and it's an honor to call him my friend.

But can you see? At that point of relational strain and offense, something bigger was on the line: namely, my call into ministry and a friendship that has, in its own way, changed many lives. Matt and I led innumerable college students to faith together over the years after that offense threatened to tear us apart.

God had an agenda: bring two people together who could change the campus.

The enemy had an agenda: separate them through offense.

We couldn't see what was on the line in the heat of the moment. But because we chose, in a way, to walk the proverbial road from Moab to Bethlehem together, and because we knew that the enemy hated it when unity carried the day, we held our friendship tighter and let our offenses go.

CARRIE

Action Principle 2:
Love Is Expensive; Be Prepared to Pay the Price

We are fools if we don't admit that valuable friendships are costly. Our friends cost us money, time, effort, and emotions. Sometimes, they even cost us our dignity. Satan loves relationships with strings attached because there is nothing farther from the gospel than loving a person only for our own personal benefit.

Ruth's promise to let nothing but death separate them was immediately tested when Naomi, more or less, called her nothing. Thankfully, Ruth refused to make everything in their relationship revolve around her need to be seen, valued, and appreciated. Again, if only this came as easily for us as it apparently came to Ruth!

The sad truth is that Morgan and I have lost friends to offenses over the years for all kinds of reasons, including our own failings. We've had friends walk away from us because they were offended by our perceived lack of commitment to fighting for social justice in our city. We've lost other friends who were offended when we took a stand against injustice in our city. If this sounds confusing, it was (and is—this still happens to us from time to time). So, which friends were right? Were we doing and saying too much, or was it too little?

We can only answer that question with another question: Did Naomi return to Bethlehem empty, or did she return with a daughter?

The answer to all these questions is yes.

From Naomi's perspective, her life was full of pain. She returned to Bethlehem with none of the fullness she carried out with her. Losing her husband and sons, her livelihood, her assumption that God would always be good to her, and her status as a married woman were all things that had happened.

But from God's (and Ruth's) perspective, Naomi's life was also full of the love of a priceless daughter-in-law. Ruth would love and serve Naomi, and God would provide the goodness Naomi longed for through that love.

She had returned both empty *and* full, even if she couldn't see it in the moment.

We have often done too little for our friends who believed a certain justice issue was the most important issue and therefore deserved our full and immediate attention. Our failure to meet their expectations has mostly been caused by the variety of work we had on our plates. We champion many justice issues to the best of our ability. We work to provide mentors for at-risk students in our local schools. We feed and care for the homeless of our city. We provide ministry to the people in our church (many of whom are marginalized in some way). We help people find therapists and counselors. We organize community groups and gatherings to help people build relational bonds around their faith. We seek to see people come out of their old lives and become discipled into a new life in Christ. Sometimes our disappointed friends have expected us to use all platforms and influence available to champion one issue all the time, but we haven't chosen to do that, and that choice has offended them.

At the same time, we have often done too much for our friends who don't believe certain social justice issues merit much concern or attention. They dislike references to those justice issues in sermons, church emails, and the organization of events specifically designed to champion a gospel-centered response in our personal lives. They see our commitment to living in the uncomfortable tensions created by injustice as an offensive dividing line between us, so they walk away.

From God's perspective, we've all done too much and too little for one another. Between the time of Naomi and our time now, humans have continually set expectations on one another that are impossible to meet. Sometimes, impossible expectations mean that by loving one friend, we offend and lose another. This is a difficult truth; love is often expensive in unexpected ways. There are still a few lost friendships we hold tenderly as we await God's restoration of all things. In the meantime, whenever possible, we choose to be a Ruth kind of friend who will pay the price when offenses arise with the hope that the relationship can thrive and grow.

MORGAN

Action Principle 3:
Be Prepared to Lament with Your Friends

Some commentators, fascinatingly, consider Naomi a female version of Job. This correlation seems legitimate since both Naomi and Job lost family members, their means of livelihood, and anything their culture considered valuable. Also, neither Naomi nor Job relinquished their faith in God even when they expressed disappointment and feelings of abandonment. Unlike her husband Elimelech, who abandoned his faith and God in a foreign land, Naomi ran home with her heartache and was honest about her plight. *God ruined me,* she said.

Before we *tsk-tsk* Naomi for calling God a life wrecker, let's take a moment to honor the counterintuitive, unexpectedly solid theology this woman was proclaiming. Naomi's refusal to blame someone else and to instead identify God as the Lord of all things, no matter what, is an example of a solid place to stand when loss arrives in our lives. Her honesty is a witness to the power of the biblical, ancient, and perhaps underused practice of lament.

People of different cultural backgrounds have different traditions and perspectives regarding lament and grief. As White, middle-class Americans, Carrie and I learned to conceal grief in our early lives. Generally, our communities considered emotional responses unnecessary and unhelpful. On one hand, this perspective can be valuable in times of severe pain and loss since it keeps us moving forward when adversity and loss arrive in our lives. On the other hand, completely suppressing our grief and emotions is unhealthy in the long run. In a church setting, our cultural "lean" created a tendency to lift our spiritual eyes above our circumstances when tragedy struck. We didn't necessarily mention tragedies in church, except to pray for God to comfort the hurting. Pain and suffering were private parts of life. We left casseroles on doorsteps, but emotional expressions were not as welcome. Our cultural perspective was individualistic in nature; we faced our losses as individuals in the hand of God.

After God grafted our lives into community with people from non-White cultural backgrounds, we learned practices that helped us lament through expressed emotions in the presence of other people. When someone from our community experienced a loss, our non-White church friends longed to grieve the loss communally on Sunday. They anticipated a collective response when grieving a police shooting, an unwelcome trial verdict, or a painful election result. These incredible people have taught us the benefit of sharing the burden of grief when lamenting all the ways the world is not as it should be. When a community grieves one person's (or one people group's) pain as its own, our souls hear the gospel in new ways that open us up to God's redemptive heart.

We needed every lesson in collective lament when our friend and children's pastor, Keivon, died unexpectedly in the middle of a church staff meeting. At the end of that traumatic day, our staff and deacons gathered for dinner at the church. Keivon was the kind of person who made everyone feel like they were better, brighter, and more talented than they had ever dared to hope before. He was a positive, enthusiastic champion of his friends' dreams. He loved to talk, listen, and connect, and we still struggle to live without his friendship.

As dozens of us sat and ate together that night, reeling from an unfathomable loss, I looked around the room and witnessed people crying, laughing, hugging, or simply sitting quietly as they tried to wrap their minds around the news. One of our community group leaders came to talk to me. He grew up across the Atlantic in a non-Christian faith. He waved his hand at the room, so full of a multitude of expressed emotions.

"This is amazing. This would never happen in my country," my friend said. "It would be only wailing. We had no hope of heaven."

He stood amazed as we lamented and mixed the hope of heaven into our pain. We didn't stuff down the pain on one hand, nor succumb to despair on the other. We believe God simultaneously wept for Keivon's loved ones and rejoiced over his homecoming. Had we only grieved privately, we would have missed out on the opportunity to witness our beloved friends' diverse ways of enduring loss and death in this life. There are no easy answers to grief, but holding one another as we grieve helps us stay connected to God.

The Naomi/Job comparison is compelling, given that Job's friends failed him. Job's friendships did not redeem his grief and loss but actually added to his pain. However, in Naomi's case, her lament that God had emptied her birthed a friend in her life at just the right time—all because Ruth didn't run when her friend's lament began. May we not, either.

Action Principle 4:
Be Prepared to Prioritize Reconciliation above Comfort

When a bank account or a bill is reconciled, it's settled. Naomi and Ruth reconciled their choices by settling themselves into the consequences of those choices, no matter what. For both of them, their choice to return to Bethlehem would result in some backs-up-against-the-wall moments. Life is rarely like a fairy tale, but Christianity insists that somehow God will one day reconcile all our grief into a happily ever after in our future. Of course, there is a lot of reconciliation and settling of bills between today and the promised happy ending. I know this from personal experience.

Once upon a time, after serving for ten years as a campus minister at the University of Texas, I was asked to move to Nashville and serve as the national director for our national campus ministry organization. Carrie and I prayed about that choice and decided the move was right for us. We were reconciled to a new life in a new state.

But then, our church in Austin called us a year or so into that new job. They were struggling, needed a new pastor, and wanted us to move back.

We began to weigh the benefits of both choices for our family: staying with the campus organization in Nashville, or moving back to Austin to pastor Mosaic. Listing the pros and cons seemed like an excellent strategy to tackle the impossible choice. That list revealed that leaving Nashville was risky. The church in Austin was fragile, and its future was unsure, with or without us. Given that I had never led a church before, there were no guarantees I would be good in that role. By contrast, I felt I was good at my job in Nashville. Nashville was stable. Nashville was a sure bet. Nashville made sense.

But when we took our pros and cons to God, he seemed to have an entirely different list of pros and cons. God held both jobs, our family, both cities—everything was in his hand. God knew the future. He asked us to open up our hearts and consider the church in Austin and how we would feel if we didn't go and the church didn't make it. Somehow, reconciling ourselves to this perspective undid all the pros and cons that seemed to naturally make sense.

We settled ourselves into the choice to move back to Austin. We reconciled ourselves to the move no matter what it cost. We put a for sale sign in front of our Nashville house and prayed to God that it would sell. Like good people of faith, we stood and believed God would bless us abundantly! (Cue the foreboding, stressful music as a montage of people not buying our house plays out in the movie version of this book.)

We lost our entire savings in the sale of that house.

Honestly, that financial loss did not feel like a ministry of reconciliation to me. But we settled into the discomfort created by our choice and signed the papers. The bank settled the rest—God bless them.

Reconciliation does not always look like shiny, happy, comfortable circumstances. Being a reconciled community of people doesn't look like agreeing about everything all the time. It doesn't look like circumstances going the way you want or expect them to go. Loving a diverse community is a spiritual decision to live reconciled to God's desire for all his people to walk in unity even when that unity creates discomfort in our lives.

Settling into uncomfortable spaces often creates opportunities to be offended (see Principle 2 again) until we remember how God settled himself into the discomfort of humanity to reconcile us to himself. After all, as 2 Corinthians 5 reminds us, God didn't count our sins against us (which would be fairer and more just) but reconciled himself to us in Christ instead (which cost him a great deal). Therefore, when the power of gospel reconciliation shapes our willingness to embrace the discomfort our differences create, our friendships become evidence of God's generosity and goodness to all of us.

Action Principle 5:
Recognize that Our Friendships Create Our Future

If we told you that your "Naomi" comes before your "Boaz," would you believe it?

Hang with us.

It's doubtful that Ruth grew up dreaming of becoming a widow, living in poverty with a Jewish woman in Bethlehem, and in the days to come, picking up scraps of grain to survive. Ruth was not living her best life. Ruth was not slaying it. Ruth's life got much worse before it got any better from choosing her risky friendship with Naomi.

When they first arrived in Bethlehem, Naomi's dismissal of Ruth implied that Ruth had chosen a terrible future for herself. But had Ruth never chosen Naomi, she never would have met Boaz in Ruth chapter 2. Ruth's future with Boaz ended up much more like a dream life than the life Ruth chose to have with Naomi. But Ruth had no idea any of that was up ahead when she clung to Naomi.

All she did was stay, despite the difficulty and personal offense. Once more, our "Naomi," our relational hard place, often comes before our "Boaz," our relational breakthrough. Staying in relationship with those unlike us, even when we are misunderstood or overlooked, can sometimes bring an unforeseen, redemptive outcome in our lives.

When we choose to be loyal, trustworthy, principled friends, we draw people toward us who value those kinds of friends, which often affords us unexpected privileges in our future. Ruth's life proves this is biblical and true. She made the right choice, at the right time, for the right reason, and her story ended better than she had dreamed all because she didn't quit on her friend, even when it looked like her friend had quit on her.

When we approach our friendships keen to any potential spiritual attack, willing to pay whatever cost necessary, with hearts full of lament for our friends' grief, and reconciled to the discomfort of forging into the future together, we find that unexpected blessings often cross our path before we even know they are there.

STORIES
from our FRIENDS

Finding Family Away from Home

BY JOSLIN JOHN

When I first arrived at Mosaic Church in 2016 after just moving to Austin, I was excited to see how diverse the congregation was. Growing up in Detroit, Michigan, I never saw a racially integrated church, with Black, White, and Latino people so connected and worshiping God together in spirit and truth. I found Mosaic inspiring and intriguing. From my perspective, the only thing missing at that time were other Indians (or Asians in general) like my husband and me!

One of the recurring events our church hosted was called "The Gospel and _____" (insert topic). These events allowed our community to explore hot topics related to current events, politics, race, diversity, etc., in relation to the gospel. At these events, we typically sat at small round tables with an assigned leader who would help facilitate discussions and ensure everyone maintained respect.

As a Spanish teacher who had also been a part of implementing diversity projects at schools in Michigan and Washington, I knew this was no easy feat. I loved that we could all listen and learn from each other without speaking over each other. Sometimes, I saw many women leading these events discouraged by what they heard, but still striving to keep these conversations going. I saw a fire inside many to see change and make an impact for the kingdom of God. I was also able to share my unique experiences as an Indian American and see people often surprised, sometimes with more questions, often with appreciation just for the sharing.

I was a part of a panel for one of these events in which I briefly shared how race and ethnicity impacted my narrative about being an American. The panel consisted of a few people who represented different races and perspectives well. I was glad to communicate my experiences of isolation and racism, as well as my fears related to raising my children without a community that looks like them. I felt that these opportunities our church created allowed many people, including myself, to learn from each other and move forward with more awareness and power.

While I have deeply missed being near my family, friends, and Indian community in Michigan, we have been humbled and blessed by the authenticity and the love of people at Mosaic. God enriched our lives tremendously as we had more conversations with people after church services, got involved in community groups, and found ways to serve and give at Mosaic. From bringing meals to our homes to praying with us, our leaders and friends have poured into us and cared deeply.

When auditioning to join the worship team, I sat next to someone whose family became our God-ordained "family" in Austin. We have walked with them through the dark and happy moments, sharing our struggles and carrying each over the past six years. I am thankful for the surprising level of understanding and comfort I've experienced in our friendship. Together, we are an example of the beauty of diverse relationships. While I am excited to see the number of Asians at Mosaic increase in recent years, I can't help but thank God for all I have learned through being stretched and put together with those who look less like me.

Chapter 4

HIDDEN GLORY

As It Turned Out

Now Naomi had a relative on her husband's side, a man of standing from the clan of Elimelek, whose name was Boaz. And Ruth the Moabite said to Naomi, "Let me go to the fields and pick up the leftover grain behind anyone in whose eyes I find favor."

—Ruth 2:1–2 NIV

As Ruth chapter 2 opens, we find that Ruth and Naomi have arrived back in Bethlehem as harvest season has begun. They have made prophetic, powerful, and principled choices to cling to one another as they began a new life. Their story is now poised to reveal how God uses our friendships and seemingly random relational encounters to shape his redemptive will in our lives.

We might miss the mysterious way God furthers his redemptive will through Ruth and Naomi's friendship with one another if we unnecessarily fast-forward through the pivotal moment when Ruth entered the budding grain fields of Bethlehem to find food for them to survive. We've discussed how Ruth overlooked Naomi's offensive disregard of her, but now we plan to peer beyond

Ruth's faithfulness to examine how, when Ruth headed out to glean grain that day, she stepped directly into God's hidden glory.

We noted in the first chapter that Ruth and Boaz eventually married and produced a son whose grandson grew up to be Israel's greatest king, David. David united the nation of Israel, settled its borders, and brought peace to the land and prosperity to the people. Even more incredible than that, David's family line one day led to another baby born in Bethlehem, named Jesus, who grew up to be our Messiah. Ruth's presence in the grain fields that day is a significant moment in her story, Boaz's story, Naomi's story, and Israel's story. But because the life, death, and resurrection of Ruth's descendant, Jesus, has qualified us to become children of God, one woman's willingness to wander into a field in ancient Bethlehem is a surprisingly significant moment in *our* stories as well.

To glean a more robust wisdom from Ruth's life, we must ask: How did God orchestrate such a grand tale? How did God shape this crucial moment in redemptive history?

Well, for starters, some might say that Ruth got a little lucky.

See, What Happened Was . . .

Let's pause for a moment, put our finger on the phrase, "As it turned out . . ." in this passage, and consider its presence and implications:

> So she went out, entered a field and began to glean
> behind the harvesters. *As it turned out*, she was working
> in a field belonging to Boaz, who was from the clan
> of Elimelek. Just then Boaz arrived from Bethlehem
> and greeted the harvesters, "The LORD be with you!"
> (Ruth 2:3–4 NIV—emphasis mine)

In Hebrew, "as it turned out . . ." means "it just so happened . . . ," which we can read as an ancient version of "see, what happened was . . ." Basically, the Bible asserts here that it just so happened that Ruth ended up in Boaz's field. Moreover, after it just so happened that she showed up in his field, "just then" Boaz arrived in the field, too. *Just imagine,* the writer of Ruth is nudging us with a wink, *two seemingly coincidental occurrences happening at once!*

Perhaps Ruth won the farm lottery?

Is the Bible offering us an ancient "meet-cute," in which Ruth picked one exact field at one precise moment, allowing God's redemptive plan for the world to transpire? Are we implying that God's plan for the world (and therefore for all of our lives) hung on one impoverished woman's singular choice one morning thousands of years ago? Are we saying God changes the world through ordinary people's seemingly random, everyday decisions?

In a word, yes. The biblical narrative in Ruth offers us no other explanation. The careful reader will note that while God's name pops up a few times in the book of Ruth, he never personally speaks or appears. Furthermore, unlike other Old Testament Bible characters, Ruth received no supernatural intervention or divine provision.

In contrast to Ruth, Abraham encountered God through the "torch and smoke" bit in Genesis 15. Moses talked to a burning bush, witnessed ten plagues, and saw God split the sea. Daniel had visions and dreams and then met an angel in the lions' den.

Ruth got nothing. No voice, vision, or dream guided her into that field. No angel warned her not to go elsewhere. And yet, God was involved in her life every step of the way.

A fuller understanding of what it means to have faith in the one true God requires that we not only acknowledge that sometimes God shows up in an evident, glorious, demonstrative way that no one can deny, but also that God's glorious and redemptive will is often revealed long after his divine, providential hand has been hidden in our circumstances. The book of Ruth teaches us not to discount God's involvement in human history, nor to erroneously conclude that God is not involved in our lives right now, no matter how distant or silent he may seem.

God has hidden his future glory in our present day, no matter if his glory is evidenced by our current circumstances. While it's impossible for us to see exactly how God plans to work in and through all the things we face today for our good, as Romans 8:28 famously promises, we can often look into the past to see how God hid his plans in seemingly trivial decisions, coincidental occurrences, or difficult seasons. One such example of hidden glory for Morgan involved, of all things, a Scantron and his choice of universities.

MORGAN

A Multiple-Choice Miracle

I became a Christian on February 26, 1995, in the A. D. Bruce Religion Center at the University of Houston. The story of how I came to stand there, sobbing in the middle of a dozen college students, may seem like pure luck, but given all we know about Ruth, there was much more at work.

I attended the University of Houston only because my junior year PSAT score qualified me to be a National Merit finalist. UH, a school I did not want to attend, happened to offer full-ride scholarships to National Merit Scholars. My parents encouraged me to take the money and run to Houston when the baseball coach also offered me a spot on the team as a second baseman. The combination of a free education plus the opportunity to play baseball at a Division I school in a great conference was too much to pass up, so off I went.

As it turned out, after I committed to going, a new head coach replaced the coach who recruited me. The new coach decided I'd make a great backup left fielder even though I had never played left field. It just so happened that the starting left fielder, Chris, was the only practicing and authentic Christian on the team. Day after day, Chris shared his faith with me, modeled outstanding character, and invited me to a campus ministry called Every Nation Campus (aka ENC).

After a semester and a half of his Christian witness, I attended an ENC meeting one night, where God changed my life forever. One of the other twelve students in the room just so happened to be a girl from Southern California named Carrie.

Long before I grasped the extent to which my future career and marital status would be radically affected by attending a Bible study meeting that night, I learned that I had scored the lowest possible score on the PSAT to qualify for the National Merit Scholarship. Imagine: had I bubbled B instead of A or C instead of D on one question on one test I took one day of my junior year of high school when I was seventeen years old, not thinking about God in the least—I wouldn't have gotten the scholarship; wouldn't have gone to Houston, which had just fired the old coach and hired the new coach who sent me to left field; wouldn't have been influenced by Chris; and therefore wouldn't have gone to the meeting where my life was changed forever. *Morgan, are you saying God's plan for your life was hanging on a standardized test version of a random coin flip one morning back in high school?* It looked that way, but it only looked that way.

When I met Chris, I was unaware that God would use our friendship as a doorway to introduce me to the gospel, redeem me from my sin, and reveal God's promise to cling to me no matter what. When I met Carrie, I was unaware that she would become the best part of my life someday, the mother of my children, my faithful ally in ministry, and the person with whom I would write a book about how God can save the world through friendships like Ruth and Naomi's. Just as Ruth walked into a field and found much more than she expected, I simply lived my life and made the next best choice, all the while completely caught up in a bigger story than I realized.

When we overlay a story like mine with Ruth's, we see how both prove God's glory hides in what seem to be the ordinary decisions we make in life. This mystery of providence is a theological point the writer of Ruth makes, and it isn't the only time Scripture employs this storytelling device. Two other powerful illustrations of God's providential nature can be found in the narratives of Joseph and Esther.

Joseph's Providential Life

Genesis 37 introduces us to the children of Jacob, Abraham's great-grandchildren. These siblings' relationships involved a mess of infighting and favoritism. Joseph was Jacob's favored son, and his brothers deeply resented him.

The sibling rivalry grew and festered until the day Joseph's brothers took their flocks to graze far from home and Joseph went looking for them. When Joseph arrived at the place he believed his brothers would be, he found a random, unnamed man wandering in the fields, who asked Joseph:

> "What are you looking for?" [Joseph] replied, "I'm looking for my brothers. Can you tell me where they are grazing their flocks?" "They have moved on from here," the man answered. "I heard them say, 'Let's go to Dothan.'"
> (Gen. 37:15–17 NIV)

Eventually, Joseph found his brothers in Dothan. In a jealous fit, the brothers threw Joseph in a pit and sold him to slavers bound for Egypt. The brothers then led their father, Jacob, to believe Joseph had been killed by a wild animal. The family's instability and problems worsened after this, exacerbated by widespread famine in the Middle East.

How would God heal Joseph's broken family and save the world from starvation (thereby keeping his promise to Abraham)? Well, for Joseph, his circumstances worsened before any hope for redemption dawned.

Because his brothers allowed hatred and jealousy to rule them, betrayal and trafficking sent Joseph into another sticky situation involving false accusations of sexual assault and an unjust prison sentence. Then one day, God helped Joseph interpret Pharaoh's dream. Called out of prison and promoted because of his wise interpretation, Joseph became a leader within Pharaoh's household, where Joseph used his governmental authority to rescue everyone, including his brothers. God wove all the heartbreaking evil that befell Joseph into a story of redemption for Joseph, his family, Israel, and Egypt. Joseph's story kick-starts the story of Moses and the exodus, which ends with God's people finding their way to the promised land. Pretty amazing stuff for a kid who was too clueless (and arrogant) to avoid his mean older brothers.

How did this whole fantastic tale start?

An anonymous man "found" Joseph wandering in a field after he "overheard" some strangers talking about moving their flocks. Let's not miss that a random relational encounter with a stranger pointed Joseph's path to the place Joseph thought he wanted to go but probably regretted in the end since it left him in a literal pit of despair.

If Joseph was anything like us, on the road to Egypt, he probably thought through all the other possible scenarios that could have happened that day. After all, had Joseph arrived in those fields five minutes later, or had the other man left five minutes earlier, everything could have been different. Had the caravan headed to Egypt taken a different road that day, Reuben probably would have fished Joseph out of the pit and sent him home to his father. Once he arrived in Egypt, Joseph's story could have ended many other ways if Joseph hadn't been imprisoned after unjust accusations of rape or if Pharaoh had refused to believe Joseph's interpretation of his dream.

The real prize for winning the "what could have happened" game is realizing that if Joseph's story had gone differently, the whole history of Egypt, Israel, and God's people would have been changed forever.

Joseph couldn't see it, but the world's rescue hung on the critical intersection of two strangers in a field, contentious sibling relationships, a boss whose wife proved reality television tells no new tales, a friendship made while in prison, unexpected favor with a king, and finally, brothers who learned from their relational failures.

In short, Joseph's story, like Ruth's, proves God hides his glory in all kinds of difficult relational encounters, as does Esther's.

Esther and Mordecai's Eventual Triumph

The book of Esther tells the story of a Jewish orphan turned "Persian Idol" winner. Theologians have struggled for centuries with her book's inclusion into the canon of Scripture because its text wholly excludes the person of God. At least in the book of Ruth, God is mentioned; in Esther's world, he appears to be completely absent.

The book of Esther tells how God once saved the Jewish people from genocide. In Exodus, God delivered the Israelites by plagues and darkness, but during Esther's life, he delivered his people through, of all things, a drunken king's relationships with his wives and subjects.

The sordid tale began when Persia's King Xerxes began to drink at a huge party. In his drunken stupor, Xerxes unwisely called for his queen, Vashti, to parade like eye candy before his government. Vashti understandably had concerns about appearing before an inebriated crowd of Persian nobles and rejected Xerxes's command. Xerxes, therefore, "fired" her as queen. This created space for Esther, a young, beautiful Jewish girl, to take her place.

Esther did not become queen overnight. Xerxes created an ancient version of *The Bachelor* and invited women from all over Persia to try to win his heart and earn the proverbial royal rose. In Esther 2:17 (NIV), we read that "the king was attracted to Esther more than to any of the other women, and she won his favor and approval more than any of the other virgins. So he set a royal crown on her head and made her queen." At first glance, the story of Esther becoming queen seems like a fairy tale of sorts. However, given Vashti's story, we know Xerxes objectified and tossed aside Persian queens as it pleased him. In Esther 2:20, we read that Esther chose to keep her Jewish ethnicity and family background a secret from everyone in the palace. This detail reveals a great deal about King Xerxes and his government. Esther was not a beloved wife who enjoyed endless favor from her husband or his subjects. Esther's race made her even more vulnerable in a palace where wives were a dime a dozen.

Given the danger, Esther's cousin, Mordecai, liked to hang out at the palace gates to keep tabs on his younger cousin and be sure she remained safe. Because Mordecai came to the palace gates on one specific day at a specific hour, he overheard (sound familiar?) a plot to assassinate the king. Mordecai reported the plot, which saved the king's life, and King Xerxes recorded the whole story in his records. This coincidental circumstance of Xerxes's favor would prove providential later, when Mordecai offended Haman, one of King Xerxes's officials. Haman's hatred of Mordecai inspired him to try to kill every Jewish person in Persia. Haman manipulated the king into declaring a governmentally authorized genocide and waited for his wrath to be unleashed on all of Mordecai's people.

When Mordecai told Esther about the plot to kill all the Jews in Persia, Esther feared Xerxes might kill her if she bothered him (again, evidence this is no fairy tale about being a princess and falling in love forever). However, Mordecai assured her that if she chose not to speak up, "relief and deliverance for the Jews will arise from another place, but you and your father's family will perish" (Esther 4:14 NIV), and then he famously suggested that she had been providentially given her place in the palace for "such a time as this."

Mordecai reminded Esther that even when an unjust person has the power to end your life, God's bigger redemptive story will prevail in the end. Esther chose to ask Xerxes to save her people, but a story of relief and deliverance for the Jews from another place unfolded along with her efforts. That place happened to be the king's own bedroom. One night, when King Xerxes couldn't sleep, he asked a servant to read from a book of records:

> It was found recorded there that Mordecai had exposed
> Bigthana and Teresh, two of the king's officers who
> guarded the doorway, who had conspired to assassinate
> King Xerxes. (Esther 6:2 NIV)

But wait a minute—the King of Persia, who presumably had the choice of an infinite number of nighttime diversions, asked to *read a book* when plagued with insomnia? And the book brought to him (he did not choose it) happened to be opened to the record of Mordecai's faithful service?

Exactly.

Shortly after Xerxes remembered Mordecai's loyal service, Esther revealed Haman's plot against her people, and a thrilling string of events began that eventually resulted in the salvation of the Jewish people from slaughter and the brutal destruction of their enemy, Haman.

But it all began when the king got drunk and made a rude request of his wife.

Once more, God's hand is hidden in the moment, but his glory is always revealed in the end. Like Ruth, Joseph, and Esther, we can't always see how God has woven our lives into his redemptive will, but we can always trust him to reveal his glory eventually. We can't always grasp how our friendships (whether challenging or flourishing) will make space for God's glory to shine out and lead us onward. It's safe to say that we may never see all the ways God is working toward something lasting and glorious through the misunderstandings, injustices, or offenses we navigate in our lifetimes.

But even when we can't see *how* God is working, God is still working.

MORGAN

Police Drama

The pain Americans (especially Black Americans) faced in 2020 following the shootings and/or deaths of Ahmaud Arbery, Breonna Taylor, George Floyd, and Jacob Blake cannot be overstated. Much of the pain and subsequent protest were aimed at law enforcement, after decades of tension and a complicated relationship, to put it mildly, between Black Americans and police.

Our city, Austin, also experienced these waves of hurt, anger, frustration, and outrage in 2020. There were daily protests, which some members of our church participated in at various levels. Unfortunately, the level of anger and frustration rose to a fever pitch at one point in the protests. Protestors congregated on Interstate 35, the main highway through downtown Austin, causing its closure. Tragically, when police used nonlethal ammunition to control the crowd, one citizen suffered a severe brain injury, and many more people ended up in the hospital. These injuries sparked more protests, anger from citizens, and by all accounts, a lot of controversy surrounding the Austin Police Department.

As we faced the pain in our city, one of our pastors remembered that a friend of his (and a Mosaic member) had met a local police chief at a gym early in 2020. The police chief had offered to help this man out if he ever needed anything. So, we called in a favor and asked the chief to participate in an online forum with racial justice activists. He agreed, and somehow, his involvement drew Austin's police chief and four other chiefs of police from surrounding suburbs to a virtual meeting where activists and officers discussed our city's challenges. The forum involved many conflicting emotions, radically different perspectives, and not much common ground. However, as a church, we were able to communicate our hope to serve as a resource capable of connecting our police force with Austin's broader community.

In the following months, the Austin Police Department continued to process the subsequent upheavals. Eventually, the police chief of Austin resigned, and the APD board reimagined their police force. A few months later, they asked Mosaic to join a new initiative spearheaded by a veteran Black officer who happened to be a Christian. This program, Community Connect, aimed to relationally connect incoming cadets with crucial subgroups of the city. APD bused 140 cadets to half a dozen venues across the city, where they listened to community leaders express their thoughts, fears, and hopes about policing in our city. Mosaic had the privilege of hosting the final day of this program. Our job was to help the cadets connect with churches in Austin. Also present that day were other APD officers and the police chief and command staff from Cedar Park, a nearby suburb.

For three hours, I joined two other Austin-area pastors on a panel addressing the cadet class. The panel was racially diverse, with one Black pastor, one Latino pastor, and me. We answered prearranged questions about how we felt APD connected with the city and how APD could strengthen its relationship with the communities we serve. The cadets had the opportunity to ask us questions as well.

During that meeting, we affirmed that APD policing needed to change to right the injustices of the past and mend the relationship between the police department and (specifically) the Black and Brown communities of our city. However, we also thanked the officers present for their work restraining evil in our city and did our best to lament the toll it took on them. We affirmed God's love for them, and we ended our time together by praying for them.

Afterward, the Black sergeant who organized the event approached me with a brilliant smile and said he didn't think it could have gone any better. The cadets later reported that this Community Connect meeting had been the most meaningful one of the week because, while the truths spoken challenged them, they also felt strangely cared for by us. I'm grateful to say we were privileged to participate in the same shaping moment for the new cadets the following year, and I hope we will continue to have this opportunity.

Now, as positive as all this may sound, we recognize we're still in the middle of a complicated story involving many layers of redemptive healing and restoration. Our citizens' relationships with law enforcement are still fragile works in progress. We await a relational miracle in the middle of the painful, often polarizing topic of racial justice and policing.

Amid our ordinary, everyday lives, God is working. His glory will eventually surface despite the suffering we've experienced, and sometimes it shows up through the pain we've endured. Perhaps, like Naomi, you've been dealt a bitter hand in our nation's landscape. If so, our prayer is that you would be encouraged by how God once worked through the disaster of famine in Bethlehem, how he worked through the scattering of Joseph's family, how he worked through the drunkenness and forgetfulness of a Persian king, and how God can work in your life as well as you step forward, in faith, into the field in front of you.

Perhaps the most amazing and encouraging thing about all three biblical stories discussed in this chapter is that they are all centered around impossible relational circumstances. Ruth, Joseph, Esther, and Mordecai endured desperate collective circumstances and personal, relational betrayal as God wrote their lives into his story of redemptive hope and rescue.

Ruth went out into fields to glean grain to survive immediately after her mother-in-law declared her as nothing (Ruth 1:21). Joseph had to figure out how to survive as a victim of human trafficking while processing the rejection of his brothers. Esther sought help from a man who valued her only for her beauty and ability to please him. Mordecai faced eradication at the hands of the king's edict while being forgotten as the one who had saved the king's life. Each move of God's hidden glory centered on a moment of tragic relational rejection in their lives.

The resolution of all three stories required a relational miracle. Perhaps we should be encouraged by this when our circumstances seem doomed without God's miraculous hidden glory, too. We will need examples like this little band of Bible heroes to find our way through our own stories, especially as we consider all the risk involved in our diverse friendships. On that note, let's talk about the risky business in the book of Ruth.

STORIES
from our FRIENDS

Facing Hard Things in Community

BY ROSALYNN SMITH, PHD

A few years ago, before the pandemic, our community group was in full swing. We gathered a few times a month to fellowship, study the Bible, and pray for one another. Our community group supported one another during hard times and celebrated with each other during happy times. We did life together. We typically met at our house every other Wednesday night. We were multicultural, multigenerational, and multiethnic. On any given night, we could easily have seven different nationalities represented. Weekly, new people showed up at our house, desiring to live in this beautiful community of people, too.

One week just before community group, my husband and I received some difficult news. A friend, a Black male, had been killed at the hands of a White male in broad daylight at a traffic light. The White man said he felt threatened by our unarmed friend. There was no fight. No threatening words are known to have been exchanged.

Our friend was a former teammate of my husband in the NFL. Our kids played together. Our families traveled together. I remember distinctly one day when our toddler boys played at a resort swimming pool together in California, and later that day, we went to see the Lakers play in Los Angeles with some other friends.

The shock of his murder hit me hard. Our Black sons were similar ages. He and my husband are of similar stature and age. My husband is a tall Black male with medium brown skin and a muscular build. He has been "mistakenly" pulled over by police more than once—in our own neighborhood.

Because the news of our friend's murder came just before everyone arrived, I had no time to cancel our community group meeting.

As we sat down to pray and study the Bible that night, I became overwhelmed. Our normal routine is to go around the room and share how each person is doing. We never got past me that night. My feelings erupted. I cried. I found myself saying the hard things that typically only my husband and I talk about when no one is around. I talked about racism, my fears for my husband and son's protection, and my fear of raising Black children in a world that does not see them as made in the image of God. I bore my true feelings about recent police brutality and killings of unarmed Black men. I expressed how I was afraid for my children to play in the front yard of our home in our primarily White neighborhood because police could mistake them as trespassers. I was angry, sad, emotional, and full of pain—and I let it all out.

That night, after community group, one of our pastors introduced my husband and me to two new couples. Both couples had brought their whole families that night, so we met the husbands, wives, and their children who were close to our kids in age. The couples were new to our church and to our community group. Our pastor pointed to the two White men and said, "Rosalynn, I'd like you to meet Officer Mike and Officer Jones.[1] They're with the Austin Police Department."

I am not sure of my facial expression or where my hands were at that moment. I only remember a hollow feeling in my gut. The room noise faded. I was numb. Then they spoke. No judgment. No harsh defensive words. No divisiveness. They didn't storm out of my house or swear revenge. They expressed their pain and desire for change in our community and our nation. We all hugged that night, and they went home.

At the next community group meeting, they returned, and they kept coming back. Now, their wives and I often pray together. Our kids play sports together and attend each other's birthday celebrations. We have not abandoned each other because it was hard. We pray about the hard. We talk about the hard. We work together to try and find solutions to the hard. Life does not stop being hard, but by God's grace and the power of the Holy Spirit, we get to walk through the hard together. I can't help but believe this is one way we can "bear one another's burdens, and so fulfill the law of Christ" (Gal. 6:2 ESV).

---

[1] Names have been changed.

Chapter 5

A HEART TO RISK

Don't Go and Glean Elsewhere

Boaz asked the overseer of his harvesters, "Who does that young woman belong to?"
The overseer replied, "She is the Moabite who came back from Moab with Naomi."

—Ruth 2:5–6 NIV

Ruth 2 shows us the beginning of a beautiful friendship between Ruth and Boaz. But within the action of this chapter, we find more than just a lovely story. As a work of literature belonging to the Hebrew narrative genre, the book of Ruth is meant to artfully capture a story that works to make a distinct point. What point does a Hebrew narrative make?

Literary works of Hebrew narrative are primarily theological, and they presume upon their readers a curiosity about the nature and person of God. The foremost goal of all Hebrew narrative—the book of Ruth included—was, and is, to ask and answer the question we see Pharaoh ask back in Exodus 5:2 (NIV), "Who is the LORD?" The answer to that question supports and shapes us into people curious about a secondary yet vital question: How should we relate to God and others?

While Hebrew narrative majors in the first question (Who is the Lord?) and minors in the second question (How should we relate to God and others?), our Western, individualistic perspective often causes us to do the opposite. Consequently, we tend to make Bible stories primarily moralistic instead of theological. We insert ourselves as the main character in the narrative, accidentally assuming the story is mainly about us, instead of remembering the principal actor in any Bible story is God. The foremost goal of these stories is not necessarily to teach us to be brave like David, courageous like Esther, or faithful like Joseph, but to gain a clearer picture of a God of grace whose interactions with humans cause us to live more wholeheartedly in the world.

Ruth 2 is a perfect place to get curious and apply the questions, in this order: *Who is God in the book of Ruth? How should we relate to him and others?* As we do this, we behold a clear view of a wide-sweeping scriptural theme: the God of the Bible is a God of covenant love.

The Hebrew word for covenant love, used nearly 250 times in the Old Testament, is the word *hesed. Hesed* is a beautifully complex word that captures what "faithfulness beyond compare" means.

The word *hesed* is used four times in the book of Ruth: twice in chapter 1, once in chapter 2, and once in chapter 3. All four uses unpack what the covenant love of God does to us. Perhaps the most beautifully complex use of *hesed* awaits us here in Ruth 2, because at its core, the *hesed* Boaz offered Ruth was rooted in personal risk and a generous curiosity.

The *hesed* in Boaz's heart began to reveal itself in Ruth 2:5 with a penetrating question. When Boaz noticed Ruth and asked his overseer, "Who does that young woman belong to?" (Ruth 2:5 NIV), this crucial question propels the narrative in a new direction. A person's family and lineage were the foundation of their identity in ancient Jewish culture. By asking who Ruth was connected to in their community, Boaz proved he was eager to know her as a person. By speaking with her, feeding her, ensuring she left with more than enough grain, and instructing his men to keep her safe, he proved he saw her as worthy of honor despite her low place in Bethlehem's societal system.

However, not everyone working in those fields shared Boaz's high regard for Ruth.

The Benefits of Risk and Curiosity

In response to Boaz's curiosity about Ruth's identity, his overseer replied, "She is the Moabite who came back from Moab with Naomi" (Ruth 2:6 NIV).

There is a whole story living between the lines of the overseer's response to Boaz's question. Boaz asked who Ruth was connected to, but the overseer chose not to answer that question directly. The first detail he offered about Ruth's identity involved a doubling down on her ethnicity: she was "the Moabite . . . from Moab." Details are often sparse in Hebrew narrative, so one detail repeated twice like this is akin to a highlighted, bolded, and italicized bit of text in a paragraph. *This is important!* the repeated detail screams at the reader. A modern day way of framing what the overseer meant could be: *She is the Nigerian, from Nigeria,* or *She is the American, the one from America,* with a suggested emphasis on *from Nigeria* and *from America* to imply a sharper, more evocative meaning of some kind. Essentially, the overseer racially profiled Ruth, intending to raise a xenophobic alarm within Boaz.

In profiling Ruth, the overseer invited Boaz to join him to do the same: *Watch out for one like her. You know, Boaz, she's not our kind.* But Boaz didn't take the bait. Instead of allowing the overseer to define Ruth using a solitary identity marker, Boaz closed the gap between himself and the woman from Moab and sought to connect relationally.

In this way, Boaz models how curiosity about strangers and people unlike us makes space for opportunities to mirror God's covenant faithfulness.

MORGAN

I experienced an opportunity to benefit from a stranger's curiosity a few months ago when I had my hair cut by a new stylist. The stylist was a kind woman in her early fifties named Michelle. As we chatted, Michelle inevitably asked where I worked, and I told her I worked at a church as the pastor. I never know where a conversation will go after this personal detail is revealed because people have a variety of thoughts and feelings about pastors and churches. Being a pastor is like being one of my kids' boxes of Legos: you never know how hard people will shake you to get a feel for what all is in there.

But Michelle just said, "Oh! That's great. Can I ask you a question?"

I assured her she could ask me anything she'd like to ask. Her first question was one I couldn't have predicted: "Do Christians believe God knows everything about us, even what we are going to do?"

I wondered, at first, if this question was some kind of trap. This kind of question usually sets up a more specific, challenging one. I am still clearly affected by my years of debate on the college campus, where many students' favorite hobbies involved asking impossible philosophical questions, like questions about God and rocks so big that God couldn't move them. But then I thought of Psalm 139:4: "Before a word is on my tongue you, LORD, know it completely" (NIV).

I answered her, hesitantly, cautiously, with "Yes."

Then Michelle asked the question she *really* wanted to ask.

"If that's true, why did God ask Abraham to sacrifice his son? That has always bothered me."

I promised her a two-part answer about Abraham but asked if I could ask her a few questions first. I was curious about this woman who was curious about God, and she agreed to a brief interview.

"Where are you from?" I asked.

"Vietnam," she said.

"Are you from a particular faith background?"

"I am a Buddhist."

"Did you know that Buddhists and Christians have a few things in common?" I asked her.

"We do? Like what?" She seemed surprised by this.

I explained that both Buddhism and Christianity seek to answer the question of suffering. The Buddha began his First Noble Truth by talking about *dukkha*, which is about seeing and considering suffering in the world. She nodded to let me know I was on the right track. I told her that Jesus of Nazareth spoke to human suffering and cared for suffering people. She said she hadn't heard that before. I then shared that both Buddhists and Christians care deeply about the subject of peace.

"Buddhism talks a lot about finding inner peace," I said as she nodded. "The Bible calls Jesus the Prince of Peace, and at the core of his teaching was an ethic of nonviolence." I proceeded to share the Christian teaching that the story of Abraham and Isaac wasn't a story about what God knew about Abraham but a story of what God wanted Abraham to know about Abraham.

Michelle had no idea what I was talking about, but I kept going.

"Let's say you are the last one cutting hair here tonight. After everyone leaves, you realize your manager accidentally left a bag of ten thousand dollars in cash on the counter. The security cameras are disabled, so no one would ever know who took the money. Would you take the money, or would you call your manager?

Christians would say God already knows what you will do because he knows who you are in the deepest parts of your being. However, you'll only be certain about who you are and how you'll respond after making your choice. So, even though Abraham had said he wanted to follow God no matter what, Abraham didn't know who he was until he faced a difficult choice that tested him."

As Michelle and I took in that thought together, I pondered how our choices in life reveal the truths about who we believe God to be and how those beliefs then shape our actions. God had sworn a covenant to Abraham, promising to make him the father of many nations through Isaac. When God commanded Abraham to sacrifice Isaac, Abraham believed that God would keep his promises. He concluded that God would somehow raise Isaac from the dead if he obeyed and sacrificed Isaac. At the core of his faith and identity, Abraham believed God was mighty, holy, powerful, and everything Abraham, as a human, was not.

Who is God? How should we live, given who God is? The answers to these questions shaped Abraham, and they shape us. We may *say* we want to be someone who loves others, no matter what. We may *say* we believe that the gospel of Jesus is not a mono-ethnic message, a generationally narrow message, or something that should be tailor-made for the wealthy. But we often find out who we really are when we walk into a room and see who is there and who is not. Who will we be when faced with the opportunity to build friendships across different lines? If all our friends only look like us, think like us, and vote like us, we may have already answered the question in a way we didn't necessarily intend. But what if we saw God as Abraham saw God? What if we knew that his covenant love could even raise the dead? We might then know God's covenant love for ourselves through the second part of my hastily cobbled together answer for Michelle that day.

"Ultimately," I told Michelle, "Abraham's story is about someone else. When Jesus came into the world, he said that all those stories in the Old Testament were really about him, that he's the missing puzzle piece."

Michelle asked me what I meant.

"Isaac didn't give his life, but Jesus did. Jesus was the Son of his heavenly Father, who came to Earth and gave his life for us. In Abraham's story, Isaac carried wood on his back up the mountain. Jesus also carried wood up a mountain when he carried his cross. Isaac survived, but Jesus suffered and died so that we could know God. The story about Abraham was really about Jesus."

Michelle considered this, and then her face brightened. She smiled and said, "I like your answer very much. Next time I want to ask you about the Passover. I don't like that story, either!"

Curiosity is truly one of God's best tools in our lives and relationships. Michelle's curiosity about my life and faith allowed me to be curious and ask questions about her life and faith. She was even kind enough to let me know what questions she would ask the next time I saw her. The type of kindness and curiosity Michelle offered me often precipitates friendship. In Ruth 2, Boaz's question about Ruth was full of curiosity and kindness. And in his relationship with Ruth, we find that friendship and *hesed* go hand in hand.

However, although Boaz was admirably curious and kind toward Ruth in the field that day, not everyone present felt the same way about her. When the overseer looked at Ruth, he didn't see a woman God deeply valued and provided for through the Levitical law. He didn't see a courageous woman who loved and cared for her mother-in-law. By seeing her primarily as a foreigner and outsider, a Moabitess from Moab, his racism blocked all possible curiosity about Ruth, her gifts, her needs, and her character.

When we discuss Boaz's lineage in the next chapter, we will understand his behavior toward Ruth in greater detail. However, at this point, when Boaz hardly knew Ruth and simply discerned that she was a foreigner, an important detail influencing his regard for Ruth was that Boaz was only half Jewish. Boaz carried a broader regard for people who were different because he was raised by parents from different races and cultures.

Boaz modeled God's deep care and concern for the underprivileged and oppressed. Our hope is that his refusal to listen and give weight to the overseer's reductive view of someone unlike him will grow our own regard and care for people on the underside of wealth and power. We also hope that Boaz's generosity toward Ruth, which set God's redemptive plan in action, will guide our own responses any time the words of the "overseers" in our culture attempt to divide us from people unlike us.

Throughout history, overseer voices have arisen seeking to "thin-slice" people demographically. These voices often consider race and ethnicity as the preeminent determiners of who we can and cannot trust relationally, spiritually, and politically. Even though our modern cultural ideals have diversified in many settings, our willingness to relate, despite differences, has often narrowed.

Allowing curiosity to draw us into conversations so we can better understand the identity markers of other people is essential if we intend to honor others as image bearers of God. However, overseers' voices and the cultural framework they create can unintentionally dismantle relationships and kill conversations. While many of those voices initially sought to elevate the stories and voices that the mainstream media has historically overlooked (which is a good and helpful thing!), sometimes those combined voices have created pressure to cut off anyone we disagree with on sensitive issues. If we allow the overseers' voices to isolate us from people unlike us, we lose the opportunity to risk personally to care for and relate to others.

Thankfully, Boaz-like hearts exist out there if we will look for them. Hearts full of *hesed* ignore the overseer's voice and, like Boaz, initiate relational connections despite (and at times even to enjoy) our differences. Boaz didn't miss the cultural consequences of Ruth's poverty, gender, or Moabite-ness. Nor did he assume he and Ruth shared the same opportunities and privileges. But Boaz also didn't allow Ruth's cultural struggles to be the definition of who she was as a person.

Colorblind: Yes, No, Maybe, I Don't Know?

In a way, the initial interaction between Boaz and Ruth bumps up against a common, controversial cultural conversation we have in the twenty-first century about the idea of being "colorblind" regarding race. At Mosaic, we have heard both White people and people of color describe themselves as "colorblind." We have also witnessed both White people and people of color take offense to the usage of the word *colorblind*. For many reasons, this word has become polarizing. Before we plunge into trying to untie the knots around the usage of this word, we'd like to acknowledge that when a White person tells a person of a different race they are "colorblind," it's usually intended to communicate respect and honor.

However, because some people of color have experienced racism from White people who claimed to be "colorblind," there lies an inherent risk of creating relational hurdles by describing ourselves as "colorblind." Anyone currently seeking to build bridges across racial lines would do well to avoid labeling themselves this way and instead simply communicate their desire to love and honor others regardless of differences. But if we allow our curiosity to lead us into better understanding the discomfort that exists around the idea of "colorblindness," we find an opportunity to connect with and honor others.

On one side of this conflict are people who believe being "colorblind" allows them to value others solely based on character without regarding their ethnicity or race. Although the intention supporting this idea can be good, two potential dangers result when we disregard a person's race and ethnicity. The first is a theological danger—namely, the loss of an opportunity to recognize how God intentionally created each of us. The New Testament in particular references people's ethnicities repeatedly to give a more robust narrative background and description of a person's identity. The second danger is cultural and relational loss. By refusing to see someone's race, we may also be (unintentionally) disregarding the benefit and beauty of their ethnic and cultural experience as well as any trauma or injustice they've experienced regarding their race. Consequently, absolute "colorblindness" can unintentionally silence the glory of God's creation, the power of our personal testimonies, and the story of humanity's failure to honor God's design and one another.

On the other hand, a perspective that pushes us to see race and ethnicity as our primary identity marker also lessens our full, God-redeemed humanity. Our identities consist of many layers and features, some of which are more significant to an individual than others. But as Christians, all other identity markers lie secondary to our spiritual identity. As the apostle John wrote, "now we are children of God" (1 John 3:2 NKJV), and our allegiance to Christ and our belonging to his family become our primary identity markers. To prioritize race or ethnicity above our identity in Christ is to lose our grasp on how God has united us as one in Christ, which consequently undermines our awareness of Trinitarian theology and weakens our relational ties as Christian people.

How, then, can we approach the idea of "colorblindness" in a more nuanced, redemptive way? How can we hold this cultural "hot potato" with grace and truth?

One suggested pathway forward would be to adopt a perspective that both "sees color" *and* retains an element of "colorblindness." We can "see color" in two ways: by celebrating the distinctive details of God's diverse design and by laboring to understand how the enemy has used physical identity markers like age, race, and gender to hurt and separate us. For example, Carrie and I carry countless stories of how our beloved Black friends have suffered innumerable indignities at the hands of law enforcement. We also deeply love and value law enforcement as an entity and the many noble police officers we know. We recognize we've never walked in a police officer's shoes nor faced the pressures and sacrifices required of police officers. However, we bear too many stories of injustice against people we love and respect to affirm that everyone is treated equally in our present day. We reject absolute "colorblindness" when we bear witness to the unique pain at the intersection of race and policing. At the same time, we insist on a type of "colorblindness" as the cure: that all people would be treated with dignity and respect by authority figures because God, the ultimate authority over creation, has made all of us in his image.

This type of "colorblindness" that honors the beauty and creativity in God's intentional decision to form every person differently is crucial for a diverse Christian community to flourish. No identity marker that exists downstream from our heavenly citizenship (Phil. 3:20) should divide us from one another. Working to honor all facets of our own identity, as well as those of others, as evidence of God's glorious design requires intentional effort but is valuable and gospel-centered. We believe God is deeply honored when we see our differences and declare they are evidence of his brilliant, intentional creative genius, all the while affirming them as less meaningful than the precious blood of his Son. By recognizing him as the author of our uniqueness, space opens between us for courageous generosity toward one another and the humility to receive from one another. By affirming God as the finisher of our faith, we overlay our differences with permanent relational glue. In other words, though I may "be from Moab" and you may "be from Bethlehem," we can still offer one another the *hesed* that Boaz offered Ruth.

> So Boaz said to Ruth, "My daughter, listen to me.
> Don't go and glean in another field and don't go away
> from here. Stay here with the women who work for
> me. Watch the field where the men are harvesting, and
> follow along after the women. I have told the men not
> to lay a hand on you. And whenever you are thirsty, go
> and get a drink from the water jars the men have filled."
> (Ruth 2:8–9 NIV)

Boaz was quick to be generous toward Ruth. He offered Ruth two privileges afforded him as a well-connected, powerful, wealthy male landowner in ancient Bethlehem. He gave her wise advice ("Don't go and glean in another field") and strong protection ("I have told the men not to lay a hand on you"). Ruth had risked her safety to provide grain for herself and Naomi. The fields were a place where women were always vulnerable in every way. This entire story, after all, takes place against the backdrop of the time of the judges, when Israel had no king and, as Judges 21:25 tells us, "everyone did as they saw fit" (NIV). Boaz recognized the possible threat to Ruth when the overseer first identified her as a racial outsider. He then risked his comfort, safety, and reputation when he chose to provide for her.

A heart full of *hesed* is a heart that desires a relationship full of God's diverse beauty. It generously offers others any privilege or provision it has in abundance. That heart communicates what Boaz communicated: *Don't glean in another field. Stay here, in this place, this space, this community, this church, with me. I'll do whatever it takes to make sure you have what you need most of all.*

CARRIE

You Can Sit with Me

Given the last few presidential elections in the United States, it seems safe to say our relational connections strain under the weight of choosing a candidate or a political party. Often, although not always, the lines dividing political affiliations run along racial and generational divides as well. So naturally, on any Sunday at Mosaic, a casual stroll through the parking lot offers a cacophony of opposing candidates on bumper stickers. We are a diverse community politically.

One of my dear friends carries a passion for justice, but politics has always been her special jam. She is a fierce and gifted leader who has patiently loved me through some embarrassing political ignorance. Her friendship has broadened my understanding of the complexities of political policy. She's the resilient, brilliant friend, and I'm the emotional, intuitive friend. But a few years ago, an election didn't turn out how she hoped it would. Some fellow church members posted aggressive sentiments on Facebook that wounded her. Those people happened to look a lot like people who had hurt her in the past, outside of our Mosaic community.

As my friend processed the consequences of the election results and the relational pain, she wondered if life and faith would be easier to navigate if she left Mosaic. How could she worship God alongside people who, from her perspective, dismissed her trauma and her past? Would her mental and emotional health improve in a church where the people she sat beside on Sunday mornings understood her better, voted like she did, and made space for her to grieve and process? This friend was not my first church friend to ask these election-inspired questions.

When my friend shared all this with me one day, my heart broke for her. I had no easy solutions or answers for her because there were no easy solutions or answers to her pain. I told her I was sorry and prayed she would hang in there. Then I promised to love her well through it all. We stayed in the field of our friendship together and gleaned from one another's backgrounds and perspectives. We empathized with one another and gained a deeper understanding of the thoughts and intentions behind our beliefs and convictions. We laughed about all the self-deprecating ways we didn't always "get" each other, and we marveled at how much we had in common.

Diverse congregations are complicated places to find peace and comfort during elections, and there is no way around that truth. This friend of mine was one of many who shared similar pain after that election. Elections demand that we decide which candidate can make our nation a better, safer, more prosperous, and just society. But we don't all agree on what creates a better, safer, more prosperous, and just society.

But if and when the people we care about feel vulnerable under any leader's authority, we can stand in the gap and promise to have their back by at least listening to them and not minimizing their concerns. We can support them spiritually, physically, and socially by praying for them, cooking them dinner on a random weeknight, and advocating for their safety and well-being. Sure, by clinging to someone "from that political party," we risk our reputation with people who "look like us" politically, just as Boaz risked his reputation by protecting an impoverished outsider from

Moab. But can we see what Boaz saw? Is it possible there is something greater at risk if we don't risk our reputation to retain our relationships?

To answer that question, we must first ask why the life of a poor foreigner mattered to Boaz. Interestingly, when Boaz offered Ruth his advice and protection, she wondered the same thing. "At this, she [Ruth] bowed down with her face to the ground. She asked him, 'Why have I found such favor in your eyes that you notice me—a foreigner?'" (Ruth 2:10 NIV).

Ruth's response to Boaz revealed the effect of a *hesed*-full heart on others when it is quick to risk. *Hesed*, or faithfulness beyond compare, elevates, highlights, and embraces the parts of us that have felt unseen or undervalued. To be clear, no friend, community, or church can meet every relational need of every person present all the time. But just as Boaz's intentional notice of Ruth validated the value she added to their community, when we validate the value God's image bearers add to our communities and churches, those spaces become relational fields where everyone can remain, glean, and grow together.

Boaz carried an awareness that one culture or perspective cannot claim a monopoly on all that is valuable in the world because Boaz was the son of a Jewish man and a Canaanite woman. We will more fully discuss the crucial complexity and spiritual significance of Boaz's family history in the next chapter, but for now, it's important to note that Boaz represented two cultures and races while maintaining an influential place in the societal structure of Bethlehem. His diverse background and complicated family story made him sensitive to the importance of elevating the oppressed and ensuring people considered outsiders could belong. Without a person like Boaz in a position of power, Ruth's story would have gone differently.

Over the years, we've found the prioritization of diversity in a leadership structure helps to ensure a community that values everyone present in a Boaz-like manner. The diversity of the influential leaders in a church or ministry should mirror, as much as possible, the diversity of its people. Although organizations sometimes use representation to promote secular platforms and ideas that might seem contrary to or set apart from Christian ideals, representation isn't a fundamentally secular societal idea or agenda. Authentic representation is rooted in the doctrine of the incarnation of Jesus Christ, which every good missiologist would tell you is the reason why the Christian faith is the most ethnically diverse in the world.

The incarnation of Jesus is the orthodox belief that God became human and came to represent God to humanity. Jesus "is the radiance of God's glory and the exact representation of his being" (Heb. 1:3 NIV). God intends this representation of himself with skin on to inspire and empower us to join God's community. We would never have known that the kingdom of God was for people "like us" had we not seen someone "like us." Seeing Jesus representing the love of God with skin on caused us to want to be a part of the larger, global body of Christ. In the same way, diversity offers an individual the opportunity to see a fully human person representing God's love for someone like them and causes them to want to be a part of that smaller Christian community. Ultimately, incarnationally-minded representations can also cause those in our cities to ask, *What could bring all these different people together?*

Given the spiritual power of gospel representation, it's not surprising that consistent, visible representation of nonmajority people groups in all levels of leadership is crucial to creating a healthy, *hesed*-filled community. There is a mutuality of benefit in diverse communities when representation is rooted in *hesed*.

Because while Ruth gleaned grain in Boaz's field, Boaz gleaned spiritual grain from Ruth's life.

Boaz replied, "I've been told all about what you have done for your mother-in-law since the death of your husband—how you left your father and mother and your homeland and came to live with a people you did not know before. May the LORD repay you for what you have done. May you be richly rewarded by the LORD, the God of Israel, under whose wings you have come to take refuge" (Ruth 2:11–12 NIV).

Here in Ruth 2:11, we learn that Boaz's generous sacrifice was inspired by a previous sacrifice: Ruth's unselfish sacrifice for Naomi. Boaz saw all Ruth risked by leaving Moab and therefore chose to risk his privilege and status for her. When he urged Ruth not to go and glean elsewhere, Boaz gave her wisdom, granted her protection, and made space for her in his life.

At the end of Ruth 2, Ruth returned to Naomi and told her mother-in-law about Boaz's words. Then Naomi exclaimed: "The LORD bless him!" and said to her daughter-in-law, "He has not stopped showing his kindness [*hesed*] to the living and the dead" (Ruth 2:20 NIV).

Boaz risked his reputation because he considered a life that displayed God's covenant love a more extraordinary privilege than his cultural, ethnic, and spiritual reputation.

In this way, *hesed* begets *hesed*. Covenant love in one person's life begets covenant love in the lives of others.

For Christians, this is a central principle on which the whole gospel stands. Christ's sacrifice reveals his *hesed* toward us and enables us to love others as we have been loved. Christ's love and faithfulness turn "outsiders" and "foreigners" into our friends and family.

Imagine what our friendships, families, and churches could be like if we showed up rejoicing in our unique differences and celebrating our mutual need for covenantal love and "faithfulness beyond compare." Imagine what we could glean from one another if we fought for everyone present to feel valued and represented, as best we could, given the demographics of where we live.

A community like that just might make a big difference in our world.

STORIES
from our FRIENDS

Conflict and Community

BY LORENA WATSON

She was afraid of talking to me. A woman I'd been friends with for several years admitted in a sheepish voice that she was scared to tell me about a decision she made that affected me. I was angry. But I wasn't angry that she'd made a decision; I was angry that she felt the need to spend twenty minutes debating with me over the phone to convince me of something she'd already decided. As a direct communicator with an internal value for respecting authority, I simply would have preferred to know the decision was made.

This, unfortunately, is one of the biggest struggles I've had in a diverse church. I am an ethnically ambiguous woman who grew up poor in the inner city. My friend is a White woman from New England who grew up in a Christian home where the culture seemed to value being nice. I'm a convert who had to learn to fend for myself in a community that valued speaking truth, not backing down from a fight, and doing friendship in a loud and lively way. After successfully leading a community group together, we found ourselves on the team responsible for organizing the unmarried adults in our church. She was the main leader, and I served on her planning team.

When we co-led our group, we'd have great conversations about how to plan and pray for the ladies with whom we spent Saturday mornings. We had lively conversations about the state of the world and how we moved in our respective workplaces to live out the gospel. But something about this assignment brought a lot of tension, and it boiled down to my style of delivery bumping up against her insecurities about leading.

What hurt the most about these kinds of disputes was that a male—regardless of race—could likely say the same things I would but not be approached with the same fear. This has been the most difficult part of being in a diverse church. We all show up with biases (me included), but my intersecting identities have a way of existing in social settings that are described by others as aggressive, intimidating, and harsh. My closest friends would say I'm honest, confident, and reasonable. It seemed wild how I felt villainized in the church in a way that I wasn't outside of it.

Fast-forward many years: thankfully, that woman and I are still close friends. I've had many other similar interactions with White men and women at my church, and I still feel loved by the people who press into the discomfort they might feel in communication while I do the same. One of my closest friends these days is a redheaded White guy who taught a class I took in which we went head-to-head quite a bit. Our conflict wasn't because I was combative; it was because I was curious, and I wanted things to make sense. Instead of seeing my passion for the things I care about as a fight to be won, this friend saw my eagerness to understand and kept at it with me. He wasn't afraid, didn't find me disrespectful, and saw a desire to engage and be engaged.

For me, a diverse church isn't about always being comfortable or changing ourselves to make others comfortable; it's about showing up with our full cultural expressions and learning to love deeply. In that security, we can live a Christian culture first.

Chapter 6

REMEMBERING YOUR TRUE STORY

The Wandering Aramean

Then she fell on her face, bowing to the ground, and said to him, "Why have I found favor in your eyes, that you should take notice of me, since I am a foreigner?"

—Ruth 2:10 ESV

What is the truest thing about you?

If you aren't sure how to answer, one way to find out is to play a game of any kind; games bring out our best and worst—and most surprising—traits.

For example, have you ever played the icebreaker game that involves taping a note card bearing a famous person's name on your forehead? One person wears the name on their forehead but has no idea who it is. The others around them offer trivia and clues about the person to help them guess the name. That game eventually separates the winners from the losers, but even more so, it creates massive divides between the extroverts and the introverts. The moment the cards attach to the foreheads, the extroverts exuberantly mingle through the crowd and joyfully interact with strangers, while all the introverts hide in the corner until someone else wins and they can safely return to their seats.

The worst possible scenario with this game is to be given the name of a famous person who is a total stranger to you. If you're told your famous person is from Minnesota, plays the guitar, and loves purple, you will never win if you aren't familiar with Prince. Or should you be too young to recall any helpful details about President Nixon, the word *Watergate* wouldn't tip you off. On the flip side, if you're too old to know that MrBeast is a massive YouTube star who also owns a chain of burger restaurants, you are doomed. This game often teaches us how many of our friends possess knowledge about hundreds of culturally, artistically, and politically important people about whom we remain clueless.

All the same, knowledge *about* a person is not the same as knowledge *of* a person. Morgan, for example, graduated from Irving High School in the Dallas area, where his school colors, he will tell you, were black, gold, and bold. He played baseball at the University of Houston and once raised his own support as a campus minister. Carrie grew up in Southern California, loves coffee, ran track at the University of Houston, and often reads too many books at one time. While these might be the details our friends would use to help someone else guess our names, they all lack the wonder of something far more important and impactful about us.

In the last chapter, we talked about the importance of seeing, valuing, and celebrating the factual characteristics and attributes that form a person's identity. But if we stop there, we might never "level up" in our relationships and learn to love the fullness of who a person is before God.

In Ruth 2, we find perhaps the greatest key to discovering how to do just that. Boaz's life shows us an exceptionally powerful element necessary for creating friendships across any kind of line. This key can talk us off existential ledges when differences strain our friendships, and it can press us to endure beyond our personal level of cultural comfort. This key can rescue us from blindness and bias, thereby making space for meaningful, lifelong relationships across all kinds of cultural lines and expected relational impediments.

What is the key to creating diverse friendships that last?

Remembering our heart's true story.

In Ruth 2, we find this key is the foundation of what enabled Boaz to relate to Ruth.

Boaz's Backstory

If Boaz were the name taped to your forehead on a note card at a Bible study you attended, you might hear the people around you trying to give you helpful details like "Jewish landowner," "older guy," or "great-grandfather of King David" to try to help you guess his name. All those might be helpful, but another, more meaningful detail gets us deeper into who Boaz was and gives us a clue as to how he was able to create and sustain a friendship with someone completely unlike him.

We've already seen how, centuries after she lived, Ruth's name was one of five women's names included in Matthew's genealogy of Jesus Christ. The five women are spread across many years, but incredibly, only our friend Boaz had a direct connection and relationship with two of the women Matthew named: "Salmon the father of *Boaz*, whose mother was *Rahab*, Boaz the father of Obed, whose mother was *Ruth*" (Matt. 1:5 NIV—emphases mine). Boaz's mother, we learn, was a woman named Rahab. Once more, names are important in the line of Christ, and women's names doubly so. Who was Rahab?

Rahab was not a Jew, but a Canaanite from the ancient city of Jericho. A great deal of ink has been spilled by religious scholars over the centuries, attempting to sort out Rahab's life and identity. In the book of Joshua, we are told that Rahab housed two Jewish spies in Jericho while they gathered intelligence about how the Israelites could best attack and sack her city. We recognize that this plot point could bring up all kinds of understandable questions about conquest, holy war, and ancient civilizations. Thankfully, helpful answers and reasonable responses to all of those uncomfortable-for-the-Western-reader questions exist in many books and scholarly papers. Unfortunately, those fascinating and challenging topics and answers lie outside the scope of this book. (Our apologies to the reader.)

However, Rahab, with all her complex and scandalous glory, is pertinent to our understanding of Boaz. One main detail about her is the thread we get to pull on from Joshua 2. The writer of Joshua introduced us to Rahab using the Hebrew words *ishah zonah*, which have traditionally been translated as "female prostitute."

To summarize, two Israelite spies came to stay at Rahab's place in the land God had promised his people. If Rahab was a prostitute, we find all kinds of fascinating questions rise again. Why *did* those two men go there to see her? Were they just looking to get away from their wives and children for a while? Did what happened in Jericho stay in Jericho? Did the men confess their true conquering intentions for the city to Rahab during a "private moment"? Or, were these spies instead morally upright men with shrewd intellects who recognized that a brothel was a far more strategic place to evade detection, given that any other men there wouldn't ask too many questions?

As scandalous as this story may seem, the case for Rahab conclusively being a prostitute is not open and shut. Some translations, for example, name her as an "innkeeper" and not a prostitute, recognizing the reality that ancient inns also frequently doubled as brothels.[1]

While James 2:25 describes Rahab as a prostitute, it's possible James was following the ancient rabbinic tradition. In actuality, all kinds of bizarre rabbinical legends became attached to Rahab's name, character, and beauty. One such legend insisted one of the effects of Rahab's legendary beauty was that even the mention of her name caused men to have a physiological reaction we've chosen not to specify here. In 2009, one group of Jewish scientists voted to rename the planet Neptune, which they decided was exceedingly beautiful, as Rahab. All of this is fascinating and somewhat odd, but the point remains that Rahab's appeal seems to defy time and logic in the Jewish consciousness.

Was she a plucky innkeeper? Was she a shrewd tavern and brothel keeper? Was she a gorgeous prostitute or a pawn in a sex trafficking ring looking for a way out of a difficult town? Or is Rahab's history some combination of these possibilities? Threads of evidence can point us in a variety of directions. While it seems most likely that Rahab was either the keeper of a brothel or a prostitute, our point is this: we want to be careful with her story and her person.

But without a doubt, we can be certain that Rahab was a racial and religious outsider from a polytheistic nation, who had heard of the Israelites with their faith in the one true God. And when she met those two men and discovered their true purpose, her part to play in redemptive history was set in motion.

In Joshua 2:8–13, Rahab explained to the spies that she had heard how God dried up the Red Sea so the Israelites could escape Pharaoh's pursuit. She had also heard of Israel's victories over the pagan kings Sihon and Og. She then told them that, at the telling

---

[1]"Rahab," Jewish Virtual Library, accessed April 5, 2023, https://www.jewishvirtuallibrary.org/rahab.

of these stories, her people's "hearts melted in fear and everyone's courage failed because of you, for the LORD your God is God in heaven above and on the earth below" (Josh. 2:11 NIV).

Rahab, instead of turning the men in, defied her king's order, lied about where the spies were, and put her future in the hands of these strangers and their God. She pleaded with the two spies to spare her and her family when the city was inevitably overthrown. The Israelites agreed, and so Rahab the Canaanite and two foreign spies hatched a daring plan regarding her future. Once Israel returned to lay siege to the city, Rahab would leave a scarlet rope hanging outside her window to ensure she and her family would be spared.

In Joshua 6:25, we're told that after the city of Jericho was taken, the spies kept their word to spare Rahab and her whole family:

> Joshua spared Rahab the prostitute, with her family and all who belonged to her, because she hid the men Joshua had sent as spies to Jericho—and she lives among the Israelites to this day. (NIV)

What happened to Rahab after that? As it turns out, Rahab was accepted into the Jewish community, put down roots, and married a Jewish man named Salmon (was he possibly one of the two spies?). Together, Rahab and Salmon produced an heir and named him Boaz.

Does this story cause you to wonder how Rahab's past shaped Boaz's understanding of the world? We certainly hope so.

How Family Forms Us

In our many years as campus ministers, we attended countless college graduation ceremonies, where we often met the families of our students. We appreciated the opportunity to tell the parents of all those students how much we loved and admired their children and to express our gratitude for the opportunity to be a part of those students' lives. Over the years, we began to see patterns of how different cultures express different values and how differently families form new generations of people. We discovered, delightfully, that for the most part, there exist two extremes on the spectrum of cultural and family involvement at graduation ceremonies.

On one end, with those from more individualistic cultures, we met many families in which (for the most part) only the parents plus a sibling or two attended the student's graduation. Occasionally, a set of grandparents might be there, or a dear friend, but for the most part the quantity of family present was small. These parents smiled and hugged their child. They clapped briefly and respectfully when their child walked across the stage and received their diploma. When we congratulated the parents afterward on their child's achievement, they politely shrugged us off, insisting their graduate had done all the work and deserved all the honor. These families were shaped around an individualistic view of people, believing that each person creates and owns their own path and successes. They were happy for their graduate, but their graduate's success did not involve them except in the vaguest nod to the way they had supported and entrusted their child to pursue their passions and goals. The story being told that day through that family's value system was one of individual success.

On the other side of the spectrum were the families from a more collectivist background. These groups gathered in large, boisterous crowds around their graduate. There was never just one set of parents plus a sibling in attendance. There were almost always siblings, aunties, uncles, grandparents, first cousins, second cousins, next-door neighbors, parents of childhood friends, deacons and pastors from their churches back home, and all kinds of other people who showed up to rejoice in what they had accomplished.

There were large banners unfurled in the auditorium. They blasted air horns and clanged cowbells from the moment their graduate stood up and throughout the entire walk across the stage. The noise rose to a deafening level when the diploma was handed to the graduate, often making it impossible to hear the graduate's full name pronounced over the sound system in the University of Texas basketball arena!

For these families, the graduation of this student whom they had loved and supported for over twenty years meant they were all graduating that day. Their collective view of family and community meant that one person's success was everyone's success. They, too, were happy about all that graduate had achieved, and they were confident that they shared in the graduate's achievement. The story being told that day through that family's value system was one of collective, or corporate, success.

Which view is correct? Are we individuals or are we each one part of a collective? We are both, of course. We are individuals uniquely created by God, and as redeemed Christians, we are part of a collective: the body of Christ.

For the purposes of our discussion of Boaz's life, the larger lesson of graduation-day families is that families shape an individual's value system along specific storylines. Our family and family's story tend to imprint on us what we believe to be the truest thing about us. Even more specifically, if we look at Boaz's life through the lens of intergenerational storylines, we might better understand how his mother's journey shaped the man he became.

We can imagine how she would have taught her son that God was mighty to save and gracious toward foreigners and outsiders. Rahab's faithfulness to ensure her whole family would be saved when Israel attacked Jericho revealed her as the kind of person who fought for her family with dogged determination. In her willingness to hide the spies and risk defying her king, we see a faith and courage that eventually made her worthy of inclusion in God's honor roll of faith in Hebrews 11.

When we flash forward sixty years after Rahab's rescue, we find her son Boaz, all grown up, looking out in his fields. When he saw a vulnerable young, foreign woman from a different racial background gleaning grain, Boaz did not just see the Moabite from Moab.

Boaz saw his mother.

Boaz's family story had come back around full circle. He remembered the story his mother would have told him: that she wouldn't be alive, and he wouldn't be here, if it weren't for the redeeming and forgiving and inclusive grace of God extended to her, Rahab, in her hour of need and desperation from someone unlike her in every way. He also remembered how his father cared for a foreign woman who, like Ruth, lived a noble and faithful story in the middle of a great trial.

When Boaz provided safety and extra grain for Ruth, his words and deeds revealed deep emotion because those words told his family's true story. Boaz hadn't forgotten the grace shown to his family. His mother's individual faith and courage worked together with the faithfulness of God and Israel to write a story that overcame her cultural marginalization. And her story had become his story any time he faced how he, too, had been born from a foreign, racially different, and (likely) sexually outcast mother. When confronted with Ruth's need, Boaz refused to be merely individualistic and say, *I have made myself rich,* or *I have pulled myself up by my own bootstraps,* or *my own hands have brought me my position and privilege and status.* He also refused to be only collectivistic by claiming his obligations to the Jewish community had been satisfied by saying, *I've done what's required of me. She can glean what's left. She's not* actually *my family. What happens to her is not my family's concern.* No, Boaz remembered his true story, and what followed was more beautiful than he could have guessed that day in the field.

Certainly, remembering our true story isn't just beautiful; it's also crucial and essential for the formation of the kind of friendships that can save the world.

MORGAN

Our Heart's True Story

Human hearts tend to forget their story over time because humans tend to forget, or to live unaware of, our inherent individual weaknesses. We resist this thought in Western society; we want to believe our achievements resulted from our willpower, effort, and dogged determination. We forget the formative part our circumstances played in our story. After all, none of us chose the century into which we were born, our place of our birth, the wealth of our parents, our talent, or our intelligence. Yes, we may have worked hard, but we did so primarily with tools and resources we did not create or conjure.

Over time, we forget that our true story isn't: *Once upon a time, an amazing human arose in the world and expressed his or her full self.* Instead, as Christians, we have been imprinted for eternity with God's own story. *Because God was gracious, he worked all things toward a majestic display of his goodness and glory.*

Thankfully, we have a God who recognizes the tendency of the human heart to curve inward and assume we're the source and center of our story. In the book of Deuteronomy, he commanded the Jewish people to recount their true story as a collective people when they stood before their priests by saying these words:

Then you shall declare before the LORD your God: "My father was a wandering Aramean, and he went down into

Egypt with a few people and lived there and became a great nation, powerful and numerous." (Deut. 26:5 NIV)

By commanding his people to identify with their nomadic ancestors—specifically, Jacob, and collectively, Abraham's family—before they presented their offering or went home approved and cleansed by a priest, God placed the story of an outsider and a foreigner at the center of their Jewish identity.

To help his people remember that God brought them out of slavery in Egypt by his own "mighty hand and outstretched arm" (Ps. 136:12 NIV), he asked them to hold their humble beginnings along with their sacrifices so they could remember that their blessings and achievements in their promised land would result from the gift and grace of a loving God.

In the same way, Carrie and I have come to see that a heart that remembers its true story is at the center of healthy relationships and fuels the vision for a multiethnic, multigenerational, socioeconomically diverse church. Without the story of how we are individuals who God rescued from our sin to give us a collective family in God, we become weighed down by the overseer's heart of fear, and we forget that we were once outsiders in need of grace. That overseer forgot that his "father was a wandering Aramean" and how God rescued his people. When the overseer looked at Ruth, he only saw the potential cost of associating with her, not the costly rescue God provided to make him one of God's chosen people.

Boaz remembered all of this—not just that his father was a wandering Aramean, but that his mother was (likely) a pagan prostitute. With nothing to stand on and nothing to boast about, when given the opportunity to extend himself and redeem a broken life, his mind flashed back to his true story. He found the courage to extend himself across racial, cultural, generational, and economic lines for the sake of one stranger's redemption because he understood that one person's redemption often has ripple effects.

If we're honest with ourselves, we will admit that our own redemption is the result of many other people's ripples.

Miracle Provision

Before I was hired as the lead pastor of Mosaic in 2009, one of our dearest friends, Brett, began a ministry to the homeless in Austin to elevate God's true story above some stories our church had previously believed. Years before, under some previous leadership, our church had valued the needs and comfort of the wealthy to the exclusion of remembering the poor. Many of us had nearly capsized in the wake of that error, and Brett decided to restore what we had lost by gathering a few folks to go out into the streets with food and supplies.

Those humble beginnings grew into years of countless truck runs stopping with supplies at gas stations, in parking lots of inexpensive motels, and under overpasses to help the homeless. Volunteers learned the names of all the people who lived under the bridges near our church facility, and they learned a lot about all that comes with not just going out to the streets, but inviting those on the streets into your local church.

The stories we have lived because we choose to love the homeless are legendary and full of tragedy at times. A transgender homeless man died on the church's doorstep during a women's meeting one night. Our on-site police officer burst into the public restroom with her gun pulled to arrest a confused man who threatened someone with a knife. Countless cups of beer have been drunk and spilled in our lobby. We often find hypodermic needles and condoms in our parking lot. One Sunday, a man suffered a psychotic episode and stood up and started shouting at me during the sermon.

We have also lived other stories. We've seen the amazing stories of personal transformation, of people getting clean and sober, getting off the streets, and finding jobs. We've been able to provide eyeglasses and dental care for many, thereby witnessing the restoration of their self-image and dignity. We've been blessed to know homeless people who live on the streets because they feel God has called them to love and serve within the community. And best of all, we have rejoiced to see many come to faith in Jesus Christ and find hope and light in God and in their spiritual family.

Recently, however, there was one story that typified the sacrifice sometimes required when the unhoused belong to and in your community. One Sunday morning, as I preached the sermon, I noticed a homeless gentleman in the back get up, leave his seat, and exit the room. Immediately, the people in the seats around his former seat began to relocate themselves. After the service, I learned the man had excessively defecated all over himself and his chair and then had gone to the men's restroom, where he had done so again. He had apparently been ill and not made it to the toilet. In an effort to clean his clothes, he had spread the mess across the walls. Once his needs were addressed and it was time to clean up, we faced a sanitation and PR nightmare.

Our incredible facilities director, Joe, humbly and a little reluctantly accepted the task of cleaning up. Joe put on a painter's gas mask and rubber gloves and got in there to restore order as best he could. However, we had to shut down our main restroom for the rest of the day, and the smell remained as hundreds and hundreds of people passed by that restroom into the main worship center. We removed the chair from the back of the room and replaced it as well.

Joe confessed later that, in the middle of it all, he wondered, "Why do we do this? Why am *I* doing this? Are we even doing anyone any good?" Joe is no ministry rookie or scared of a tough moment—he has lovingly cared for countless unhoused people in all sorts of challenging conditions. But it was a low point, without question.

Let's ask Joe's question. If caring for the unhoused is risky and impossibly costly, *Why do we do this?*

Other church members have asked the same question over the years, and the discomfort of a visible homeless presence within our larger church community has caused them to leave Mosaic. The ensuing leadership lesson for us has been that, as church growth strategies go, welcoming the unhoused into your community does not support massive multiplication, nor does it fortify your financial situation. The bottom line? Loving the poor and financially marginalized is risky. When housed, financially stable people leave a congregation because the number of unhoused people present on a Sunday has grown to cause them discomfort, their financial contributions (which help fund the street ministry) leave with them. The difficult truth is that, for those of us who live under roofs behind doors that lock, street ministry isn't something we only do "out there" under a bridge, but "in here" within our hearts and the walls of the church facility.

Serving unhoused people can't be considered a church growth strategy in the traditional way leaders might desire to see growth, which usually hinges on numerical values (attendance, baptisms, membership, volunteer numbers, etc.). However, loving and serving the homeless and less financially stable people of your city will grow a church to love the gospel in greater measure 100 percent of the time if the people served are treated as beloved friends who are worthy of dignity and care no matter what they may lack materially. As we pursue these friendships at Mosaic, God sometimes shows up to remind us that his gospel love for all people is even bigger than we previously assumed.

Recently, I received an unusual voicemail that seemed too good to be true. On the recording, a pastor from another part of our city, whom I did not know, said his church was struggling and he planned to retire. He and his leaders were considering what to do with their fully paid off and debt-free eight-acre facility on the other side of town—and they wanted to gift it to us.

Had I misheard what he said? Was I being pranked by an old friend with a fiendish sense of humor? In the middle of an Austin real estate market that had lost its mind, in which we could never dream of acquiring even a tiny storefront property, this pastor's generosity seemed impossibly ludicrous.

When I called him back, he confirmed I was not being pranked and that I had understood his intentions perfectly. I asked the same question Ruth asked Boaz when his offer to protect and provide for her exceeded typical generosity and that our facilities director asked himself when his service that disgusting Sunday exceeded anyone's comfort level: *Why?* Why would you do this? We are strangers. We've never spoken or seen each other before. Why us?

Then he said, "It's because your church serves the homeless."

As it turned out, his congregation also had an ongoing ministry to the homeless community in South Austin. Apparently, one day, one homeless man showed up to receive their help. When they invited him to come back on Sunday, he politely declined, telling them, "Mosaic is my church home; I feel welcomed there." As it turned out, that Mosaic member was the same man who made the catastrophic mess in his seat and in the restroom that one Sunday.

Suddenly, the ridiculous grace of God struck my heart. Our steadfast commitment to love and serve people who have so little and to sacrifice so we could remember our true story had resulted in a more generous provision than we could've imagined. God did for us, through the friendship of one of our homeless friends and the extraordinary generosity of others, what we could not have done for ourselves.

Spiritually, we all share the same true story, and it is the story of a person who couldn't make it to the bathroom quickly enough to avoid creating messes others must clean up. We are people who did not have a home of our own to hunker down where we could save ourselves from needing rescue and salvation. We needed help and care and a place to belong.

In the end, our father was a wandering Aramean named Abraham. His father worshiped idols and rejected God. But God, rich in mercy, spoke to Abraham, saved him, and eventually, Abraham's family line produced the ultimate outsider, our Messiah, Jesus. Jesus became the scarlet rope that hangs outside the window of this world so that all who call on his name will be spared from the just wrath of God and be welcomed into a new family. The Son of God showed up, cleaned up our mess, and invited us into his Father's house, where he clothed us in his clean and righteous robes.

When someone faced with the mess and inconvenience inherent to sacrificially serving others asks why we care for the homeless, focus on young people, provide for strangers from other nations, or bring people of different backgrounds together, I fear their hearts have tragically forgotten the grace of God.

Our hearts shrink when we forget our true story. But once we remember it, our lives begin to echo Boaz's words to Ruth: *Don't go away from here. Come stay in these fields. It will be better for you here. Your life can be redeemed because we're better together.*

There is a kind of note card on your forehead with a name on it, by the way. That person's life reveals the truest thing about you.

His name is Jesus.

STORIES
from our FRIENDS

Relating in Relational Diversity

BY KEONG FONG

Migrating to the United States from Malaysia at the age of fifty-three was a big step. My family and I experienced the impact of being dropped from thirty thousand feet into a new country and culture.

It wasn't as significant a change as we thought it would be. Possibly, this is because we live in a world where we share similar experiences and are exposed to US culture in all its forms. There are McDonald's, Starbucks, and Pizza Hut outlets everywhere, all over the world. We predominantly watched US movies and television series and were immersed in many aspects of US life. It feels like the US culture has the highest level of international exposure.

However, as we began to integrate with US friends and neighbors, we discovered that the things that set cultures apart are the subtle differences, not the large and obvious ones.

Something that stood out for me is that different races have different accents in Malaysia. In the United States, everyone sounds the same to us. While the different races here may see diversity among themselves, foreigners see Americans as one culture and one people. I feel like I'm from a different culture because of how I speak and think.

One aspect that helped us assimilate into this new country was finding a church we could belong to. Even then, it took us months of visiting many churches before finding one where we felt welcome. At Mosaic Church Austin, people came up to our family to talk with us and made us feel welcome. We began to involve ourselves in church, a community group, and street ministry. An interesting turn of events occurred when Pastor Morgan asked me to apply for the director of connections position, as he felt I would fit that role.

I was welcomed into the church office by the warm and loving people that make up the staff of Mosaic. I was the first non-American and also the first Asian on the team. Every staff member truly welcomed me, but I still felt on the outside, looking in, not catching the cultural context of jokes that people laughed at and not understanding the sports references. This is not because I was dealing with prejudice, but because I do not share the cultural history of being an American. I realize that this is something that will never change. I cannot adopt a history that I don't have.

I felt like an outsider, even though no one made me feel that way. Then, at one staff prayer meeting, a brother released a word from the Lord to me. He said, "You should know that you are a part of Mosaic and do not doubt that God has a message that he wants to deliver through you. Persevere in what you are doing."

My heavenly Father knew exactly how I was feeling and wanted to assure me that I am where he wants me to be. Yes, there will always be cultural differences, but I should not consider that as cultural rejection. This word from the Lord also encourages me to share my thoughts and opinions, even if they differ from what my friends say. Willing, open discourse should be a two-way experience. My brothers and sisters should also not hesitate to press into topics they do not understand just because we are from different cultures.

God has made us different, yet his Holy Spirit unites us in ways that bring richness to us and glory to him. Our differences help us understand God's purposes better when we press into them and allow that diversity to truly make us citizens of God's kingdom.

Chapter 7

THE COMFORT OF FRIENDSHIP

Finding Rest for One Another

One day Ruth's mother-in-law Naomi said to her, "My daughter, I must find a home for you, where you will be well provided for."

—Ruth 3:1 NIV

In 2020, humankind watched 57.1 billion minutes of the television show *The Office*.[1]

For perspective, one year equals 525,600 minutes. Therefore, we collectively watched more than one hundred thousand years of Michael Scott, Dwight Schrute, and Jim and Pam in one calendar year of existence. Take that, COVID-19.

To be sure, we watched other shows and movies that year in vast quantities as well. During the lockdown, "comfort television" became a way to cope with the mental and emotional stress of the pandemic. *Friends* was the most watched show on HBO Max, and researchers estimate we watched 96 billion minutes of Joey,

---

[1] Adam Bankhurst, "*The Office* Was Reportedly 2020's Most Streamed Show," *IGN*, January 13, 2021, https://www.ign.com/articles/the-office-was-reportedly -2020s-most-streamed-show.

Chandler, Ross, Phoebe, Rachel, and Monica in 2020.[2] And even amid an international health crisis, viewers couldn't get enough of *Grey's Anatomy*. It was the second-most streamed show that year.

These shows made space for us to: (1) remember that the world hadn't always been this crazy while we (2) watched well-worn storylines work out in the end (again), despite (3) the precarious middle parts of their narrative arcs, and (4) hope that our stories were also racing toward a better ending than we could see at the time.

Yes, we abundantly escaped into worlds that still provided toilet paper for their occupants and where people weren't punching each other over masks. But it was more than just familiarity we were after. When our world seemed devoid of comfort, and when we were isolated from dear friends and relatives, many of us turned to old, familiar television centered on one specific theme. We consumed billions and billions of minutes of familiar stories centered around this one central theme when we felt desperate for proof that things would work out in the end.

That theme was friendship.

We reached for how television friendships could grow, struggle, and prevail in a time when our own friendships seemed to crack under the increasing isolation, polarization, and social media bloodbaths that 2020 brought us.

But where are we now, and what have we learned? The pandemic drama has died, but where did we land? How did everything work out in our friendships after the pandemic? After our disconnection from people we loved, did we learn how valuable our connections to one another are? Or are we stuck in "season two"

---

[2] Josh Kurp, "*Friends* Fans Spent a Staggering Number of Minutes Watching the Show on TV Last Year," *Uproxx*, March 19, 2021, https://uproxx.com/tv/friends-pandemic-viewership-nielsen-ratings/.

of a relational tragedy of some kind, still waiting for someone to fix the plot holes?

How can we, the people God has called his friends (John 15:15), live as those who love not only the people who love us first but even people who might consider us their enemies (Luke 6:32–36)?

Perhaps we can find the path forward in friendship if we will slow down for a moment to see what Naomi did in "season two" of her own relational story, which is where we find ourselves at the beginning of Ruth 3. Ruth 3:1 is the center of the Ruth narrative, and it reveals how to succeed at friendship when the world is falling apart.

At this point in the story, Ruth arrived in the barley fields and met Boaz, who welcomed her to come back. After a successful day of gleaning, Ruth returned and reported on all that happened in her courage-filled quest to provide for Naomi. And when Naomi saw how Ruth had provided for her, she responded with her own words of friendship.

Naomi said, "I must find a home for you, where you will be well provided for" (Ruth 3:1 NIV). The Hebrew word for home is frequently translated as *rest*, and it is the word *manoach*, which implies the comfort of security and tranquility. Interestingly, Naomi also used this word in Ruth 1:9, when she said to both Orpah and Ruth: "May the LORD grant that each of you will find rest [*manoach*] in the home of another husband" (NIV).

In chapters 1 and 3 of Ruth, Naomi was the person who used this word. Despite her total lack of comfort, she twice advocated for the welfare of her friends from a desire to provide the *manoach*, or comfort, she lacked. The restless and empty woman insisted she had to be the one to provide rest and comfort for her friends.

We should commend Naomi for not allowing bitterness to taint her hopes for Ruth. Naomi's generous friendship proved she hadn't relinquished all hope for redemption even after losing her comfort and security and renaming herself "bitter." She didn't become permanently jaded and suggest that all marriages would end in sorrow and despair as hers ended. Naomi hadn't deconstructed her life to the extent that left her with nothing to offer when Ruth needed wisdom and guidance. Despite all she had gone through—first on the road back to Bethlehem, and now here with a man like Boaz in view—Naomi told Ruth, both times, there could still be *manoach* in her future. Naomi said, *I want to be the friend who helps you experience rest and tranquility.* And then she went for it. Naomi didn't just talk about it—she made a plan to find it.

While Ruth would be the one to carry out her mother-in-law's unusual plan, this plan (we'll see it in a moment) had high stakes and a high possibility of failure, and any negative consequences would have affected both Naomi and Ruth if the plan had failed. This story proves that friends who advocate for one another's rest while risking for another's welfare transform our lives and communities. Simply put, the best friendships involve equal parts rest and risk.

MORGAN

Rest + Risk = Formative Relationships

Carrie and I were friends for six years before we began dating. For many years, whenever someone would ask why we hadn't dated yet, since we were such good friends, I had only one reply. "I could never marry her; she's too good for me. I would love to marry someone like her, but I don't want to ruin her life with all my stuff." When those same people asked Carrie about our relationship, she more or less said the same thing.

Without fully realizing it, we both longed to see the other person find someone who offered them *manoach*; we hoped to see the other person attain a future rest that we were afraid we couldn't provide ourselves. In many ways, this was why we were such good friends. My (relatively) selfless faith (in this instance) insisted Carrie deserved to be loved and safe, which created a kind of comfort in our friendship that made space for her to be herself around me. Her similar regard for me communicated that I had nothing to prove to her, which ironically also made me think she deserved someone better than I could be on my own. It took us six years to understand that our deficiencies and weaknesses wouldn't ruin the other person's life. Ironically, we needed the wisdom of a kind of Naomi to figure it all out.

That wisdom came to Carrie one night in a diner in Studio City, California. Carrie told her mentor, Sandy, about how our friendship had begun to feel different to her. Sandy asked if Carrie thought I felt the same way, and Carrie mentioned I had asked a strange question the last time we talked.

"He asked me how much debt I had," Carrie said.

(I know, I know. Not the smartest nor most romantic question to ask. But in my defense, it did get the ball rolling.)

Sandy, thankfully, knew I was a fairly impoverished campus minister at the time and correctly deduced my fiscal nosiness was a good sign, proving Sandy had earned the right to be called a wise mentor. Since I had been the nosy one, Sandy suggested that Carrie call me and ask me to fess up about how I felt about our relationship.

"If he says he wonders if you could be more than friends, tell him you feel the same way. If he says you're just friends, and that's all you'll ever be, tell him you feel the same way."

It was brilliant. Either way, our friendship would be safe, and therefore, Carrie and I would be able to continue to find rest in it. Carrie called me and risked rejection. I risked and shared my true feelings. Our story as more than friends began.

Years later, reading Naomi's plan in Ruth 3, it's easy for us to imagine Sandy filling in for Naomi in the scene when she hatches her plan to help Ruth find a future full of *manoach*. Just as Sandy hatched a plan for us, Naomi hatched a plan for Ruth and Boaz, and here it is:

> Tonight [Boaz] will be winnowing barley on the threshing floor. Wash, put on perfume, and get dressed in your best clothes. Then go down to the threshing floor, but don't let him know you are there until he has finished eating and drinking. When he lies down, note the place where he is lying. Then go and uncover his feet and lie down. He will tell you what to do. (Ruth 3:2–4 NIV)

Naomi's plan risked Ruth showing up and making herself vulnerable to a man she barely knew. But just as Sandy used my nosiness as a clue to my intentions, Naomi considered Boaz's history of kindness toward Ruth when calculating Boaz's potential response.

Many people have regarded Naomi's plan as a "Ruth gets extra saucy" moment in the Bible. They've interpreted Naomi's advice as instructions to seduce Boaz to (hopefully) get Ruth pregnant, which would trigger Boaz's financial involvement in their lives. After all, Naomi's plan involved suggestive details: it happened at night, in the dark, after Boaz had been drinking a bit, and it hinged on his response to discovering a beautiful young woman at his feet. The result could have gone lots of ways—and Naomi knew this. She even left Ruth with, "He will tell you what to do." Naomi's plan didn't exactly put the ball securely on the tee for Ruth.

And yet, as modern readers, we must remember how few paths forward Ruth and Naomi realistically had as poor widows in the ancient Middle East. As modern Western people, we enjoy privileges like education, access to basic needs, and stable societal structures that provide access to paths and opportunities Ruth and Naomi could never have imagined. Humbling ourselves before asserting what plan we might roll out in a desperately vulnerable moment will help us move closer to God's merciful favor toward Naomi and Ruth.

But grace and humility aren't the only attributes capable of enlightening us regarding the morality of Naomi's late-night instructions to Ruth; knowledge and education also defend her. Despite any sermons you may have heard that insinuated that Naomi told Ruth to manipulate Boaz sexually, many Bible commentators don't believe Naomi's plan promoted some low kind of sexual morality. For example, in his book *Strong as Death Is Love*, Old Testament scholar Robert Alter writes that Naomi's plan aimed to help Ruth communicate to Boaz her understanding that a wife's place in their culture involved submission and even subservience to her husband. According to Alter, Naomi's instructions for Ruth to wash and anoint herself with oil communicated her intentions to be pleasant and appealing to Boaz.[3]

But still, it was an enormous risk and could have gone sideways quickly for all involved.

Naomi and Ruth decided to shoot for the moon and reach for the rare opportunity before them: a compassionate, generous, wealthy man from Elimelech's own family who could legally restore their land and continue Elimelech's family line by marrying Ruth. If the plan worked, the resulting rest and comfort they reaped would be a rare miracle well worth the risk.

---

[3] Robert Alter, *Strong as Death Is Love: The Song of Songs, Ruth, Esther, Jonah, and Daniel: A Translation with Commentary* (New York: W. W. Norton, 2016).

A Rare Relational Blessing

Morgan and I have hosted a church community group in our home for many years. We've had countless people carry a plate of cookies or a casserole into our home, place it on the big pot-luck island, and join us in sharing our lives, thoughts, needs, and laughter. We have witnessed babies born (though not in our home, thank goodness), weddings planned, children sent off to college, and promotions attained. We've lamented illnesses, accidents, job losses, and tragic deaths. But mostly, every other Sunday night for over a decade, a dozen or more kids have hung from chandeliers (not really, but close) shooting Nerf darts at each other while the adults discussed their faith in the living room.

A few years ago, hosting our group in our home became a little too stressful because of some of the circumstances in our lives. We rearranged our group, sent out some incredible leaders to begin a new community group in their home, and then moved our meeting to another home for a while. We enjoyed our respite from the biweekly chaos in our house. But toward the end of 2019, Morgan expressed a desire to start a new group in our home again.

I was not on board. I was still basking in my hiatus from scraping cupcake frosting off the playroom ceiling and keeping a lost and found box full of socks, water bottles, and pie servers. Morgan smiled at me and promised he believed this was the right thing for us to do. He was extremely convincing, but I pretended I didn't understand any of the reasonable, heartfelt reasons he offered because I didn't feel a personal need to host a group and was happy in our life at the time. Besides, I argued, our living room furniture had been demolished by our old groups, and where would people sit? After much deliberation, discussion, and negotiation, Morgan got a new community group, and I got new living room furniture for that new community group to ruin. This is how our marriage works, I guess. I'll leave it to you to decide if it makes sense.

From our first Sunday evening together, that new group felt unique. We were diverse in countless ways. Some of us were single, others married without kids, and others married with kids. We were a mix of races, White, Black, Latino, and Asian, as well as a mix of nationalities, American, Filipino, Canadian, and South African. We were male and female extroverts and introverts, of different political ideologies, raised in church or newer to the faith, and from different generations. In this new group I experienced an immediate, strange kindness and hospitality that felt like coming home while I was actually in my own home. As an introvert, I often feel uncomfortable in larger groups of people. But in that group, I found a *manoach* kind of rest.

Then one night, as our whole community group sat around our living room, our friend Jeremy expressed concern that a virus making the news in China would become a huge problem. We all nodded but secretly thought Jeremy was exaggerating things a bit. Of course, Jeremy was right.

Over the ensuing months, as we gathered virtually instead of in person, the *manoach* of that group became a lifeline to Morgan and me. It would be easy now to downplay how desperately lonely we felt during that time. Groceries were challenging to find. No one went to work or school. We canceled all our plans and trips, and we lost some of our hope with those cancellations.

We all felt bitter and empty in one way or another. I remember the loneliness of the single people in our group, who hadn't been physically present with another person in days, then weeks, then months. I recall the specific strain of toddlers on parents trying to work from home. I remember the fear we fought back with our faith as we looked to God, as Naomi once looked to him, as the only one who could stop all the suffering.

I don't want to forget our desperation in 2020 because the rare blessing of being loved by those people saved us from despair many times that year. Morgan had been right; we *had* needed to start a new community group in 2019. But we hadn't realized the new group would offer us a rare kind of relational resource in 2020. The old world burnt to the ground as we faced all we faced and as we struggled to process the loss of the lives we had always known. But the twenty people on our computer screen still loved one another, and their love for one another caused our hearts to hope that God's grace hadn't finished our story yet.

We often must accept what we get in life, whether it seems like enough or not, whether it seems deserved or undeserved. We get to host the group we want to host and it goes just fine. We buy a new sofa for the group to sit on and the story ends there. But every once in a while, grace offers us unexpected provision through a room full of people who love us for who we are, not for what we can do for them. In the middle of the most brutal year of our lives as pastors, when we were weary and worn down to nubs, our community group gave us themselves, as best as they could, and when we tried to reciprocate the love equally, they laughed and said our friendship was enough. The *manoach* they offered us only heightened our desire to provide rest, tranquility, and comfort in return. When you find friends like that, by the way, hold on to them as tightly as possible.

And yet, we can't stop there, because *manoach*-like rest also requires an equal portion of risk—and sometimes, truth be told, the weight of the risk is not evenly distributed.

Tallying Things Up

Have you ever wondered what Ruth first thought when Naomi presented her threshing floor sleepover plan? Although the text indicates Naomi intended to be a good friend and good mother-in-law by finding rest for Ruth, this idea about sneaking into Boaz's sleeping quarters and lying at his feet involved a whole new level of risk. And as we indicated earlier in this chapter, if the plan went to pieces, Naomi's future prosperity would be jeopardized, along with Ruth's. However, we must acknowledge Ruth's burden of risk exceeded Naomi's, because while asking Boaz for so much meant both women risked losing their access to grain and ruining a unique opportunity for redemption, only Ruth risked humiliating rejection, a bad beginning to a marital match, and her physical safety that night.

Clinging to faithful friends who benefit you greatly in the middle of hard times makes sense. Risking for the sake of people who have never hurt you seems logical. But can we make sense of Ruth's choice to follow the plans of a woman whose words and actions insulted and cost her so many times?

We don't know for certain if Ruth kept track of all the offenses Naomi committed over the years, tallying them up. However, we do know *someone* kept track of the offenses that happened in Bethlehem, since they were recorded here in this ancient text. Let's create our own tally sheet, shall we?

When Naomi shooed Ruth away on the road to Bethlehem, Ruth refused to take this personally, become a victim, and say, "Well, if you don't want me in Bethlehem . . ." or shoot back to protect herself with something like, "I was only going so you wouldn't have to be alone!" When they arrived in Bethlehem and Naomi completely dismissed Ruth as nothing instead of introducing her to the town, Ruth didn't accuse Naomi of being ashamed of having a Moabite daughter-in-law or slap Naomi and tell her to wake up and remember Ruth's loyalty and devotion. When their survival relied on gleaning grain with the lowest of the low in society, Ruth didn't insist Naomi join "Team Glean," nor did she take it personally that Naomi stayed home all day while Ruth labored in the fields, even risking sexual assault.

To tally the offenses Ruth overcame to remain with Naomi is to realize that Ruth carried the greater burden of risk and work in the relationship. There is no evidence in this story that Naomi risked her physical safety to remain in relationship with Ruth. Possibly, returning to Bethlehem with a foreigner could have brought social scorn upon her, but Naomi distanced herself from that outcome by declaring she returned with nothing. Any xenophobia felt by judgmental Bethlehemites could have been cooled by the possibility that Ruth followed Naomi all the way from Moab without Naomi's consent.

In this modern era, many voices tell us to cut people out of our life if the relationship feels one-sided. Those voices say that anyone who doesn't add value to us, make us great, or help maintain an unbreachable circle of positivity doesn't deserve our time, effort, or resources. Was Ruth's willingness to love and serve her broken mother-in-law to her own potential detriment a sign of weakness or a sign of strength? Was Ruth's loyalty the source of her greatness, or was it the bullet she dodged because all's well that ends well? We wholeheartedly acknowledge that sometimes we must distance ourselves from abusive people and end abusive relationships. We also acknowledge that establishing healthy boundaries is one way to be a good friend. But Ruth's story reminds us that loving a friend through a season in which they are emptied by loss and grief is not a sign of weakness, and it also reveals the spiritual nature of our earthly friendships.

The eventual happy ending of Ruth's loyalty to Naomi reveals how our fidelity is spiritually weightier when our friend does not deserve it. Somehow, long before her future descendant would walk the earth, Ruth embodied the words of Jesus in Luke 6, when he declared that loving someone who loves us back is no credit to us at all. That's called easy love. Not even the worst people struggle to be friends with people who make friendship easy. Case in point: Naomi didn't struggle to love Ruth because Ruth made Naomi's world a better place! But can we befriend someone who seems to offer nothing in return? Can we love a woman who tried to send us away, told her friends we were nothing special at all, leaned on us for her survival, and asked us to propose marriage to a rich landowner in the dark of night? According to Jesus, that's the way to find a real reward:

> But love your enemies, do what is good, and lend, expect-
> ing nothing in return. Then your reward will be great, and
> you will be children of the Most High. For he is gracious
> to the ungrateful and evil. (Luke 6:35 CSB)

Jesus did not say this as a person unaware of how little value his friends would be able to offer him personally. When Jesus said access to a spiritual reward relied on loving our enemies, he spoke of the full relational burden that would one day fall on his own shoulders so that we could be called children of God. Therefore, perhaps our reward for loving our enemies and our difficult, empty friends is an opportunity to inherit the kingdom of God in new ways.

From Jesus and Ruth, then, we learn that loving our friends beyond their worthiness and without regard for personal benefit allows us to participate in bringing God's kingdom on Earth as it is in heaven. After all, without Ruth's near-scandalous devotion to Naomi, these two women would not have been included in God's salvific plan for the world, and the lineage of the Messiah would have had to be woven another way. And without the scandalous grace God offers us through the cross, we would not be coheirs with Christ deemed worthy of eternal life in God's kingdom.

Our burdensome, difficult friendships often become the places we encounter God's kingdom in new, life-changing ways when they cost us more than we expected. We can think of one heavy friendship in Morgan's life that illustrates this perfectly.

MORGAN

Dirty Shirts and Missing Groceries

When Jesus saved me in college, he gave me an incredible gift by placing me in a campus ministry where I met James (not his real name), a student different from me in every possible way except for our shared faith in Jesus. This relationship, in its beginning, felt risky and not relaxing.

Somehow, James and I ended up as roommates in the Third Ward of Houston, Texas. He proceeded to inform me that I represented everything wrong with the world. James actively disliked and insulted me, yet he also regularly asked me for a late-night ride home from his job as a waiter after his car broke down. Go figure.

Many nights, as I drove him home, James insisted our friend group was racist, which was hard for me to hear. Although we were an ethnically diverse crew at the time, James was unlike anyone else in the group. I often arrived home after class to find James had helped himself to my food, worn my white dress shirts to work without asking, and discarded those shirts on the floor of his closet, stained and dirty. When I confronted James about eating my food and wearing my clothes without asking, he called me selfish. James did not seem to be one of those rare, grace-filled community group friends Carrie wrote about earlier in this chapter. To be friends with James cost me a great deal and made me very angry.

It seemed impossible to maintain a friendship with James. However, our conflict exposed the depths of my heart as James and I began to have challenging conversations about culture, race, privilege, and power. He shared astonishing, heartbreaking stories about how law enforcement had treated him, the lack of a father in his life, and his mother's suicide. I realized that if we compared our pasts, almost everything that had been wrong in his world had been right in mine. Our conversations changed our regard for one another, and the tides of our relationship began to shift.

James stopped eating my food without asking, and I started sharing my food without being asked. Our friendship cost us our assumptions and biases, but paying that price increased the value of our faith in God and one another more than we imagined back when I raged about dirty shirts and missing groceries.

When I hear Christian people say that multiethnic friendships don't work, I know they're wrong because James's friendship became a gift to me. But also, I assume they've never read the book of Ruth with an accurate understanding of the value of the multiethnic, multigenerational friendship Ruth and Naomi shared. Even more, I wonder if people who think it's too challenging to befriend people from different ethnic, generational, cultural, and socioeconomic backgrounds have read the Bible in its entirety. It seems they have somehow missed that Jesus chose to call them his friends despite their lack of similarities with the Son of God.

The question we face in diverse friendships is not "Can we pay the cost of befriending people unlike us?" but "What will we miss out on if we *don't* pay the cost to befriend people unlike us?" Because the truth is, God shaped history through Ruth and Naomi's friendship and has continued to use friendships to shape the world ever since. The friendships we form today shape the world we live in tomorrow. The rest we offer one another now and the risks we take in love pave the way for a breakthrough later. I once learned this up close and personal at the elementary school around the corner from our church.

Nothing Left to Lose

Several years ago, a group of pastors here in Austin asked the superintendent of schools what they could do to serve and impact local public schools most significantly. The superintendent explained that early student literacy is the key to lower dropout rates and success later in life, and he shared the single most effective solution churches could offer to help solve that problem.

"We need mentors to help establish a value for reading," he said.

When I heard this, I knew I wanted to be a mentor, and I felt confident many people from Mosaic would feel the same way. I picked up the phone and called the elementary school nearest to Mosaic and asked to speak with the head counselor. I told her Mosaic wanted to send as many mentors as possible to support their campus and asked to meet with her to discuss the details. In the following weeks, the counselor opened the door for our mentors to go through the district's training and matched each mentor with a student whose parents had requested help.

I'll never forget the morning the counselor called me, saying, "I have a first grader for you to mentor. Last week, his father died of a heart attack in front of him and his brother, and he's really struggling. Would you be willing to mentor him?"

I said yes and went to the school the following week to begin a relationship with a student who would come to change my life over the next eight years despite a bit of a rocky start. Henry[4] and I shared little in common. He was from an ethnic and cultural background unlike mine, was thirty years younger than I, read below his grade level, and we shared very few similar interests.

During the first year of our weekly thirty-minute meetings, we mostly played card games and made stuff out of Play-Doh.

---

[4] Name changed for anonymity.

Any time I suggested reading a book, Henry declined. I felt the clock ticking on his literacy level. As the son of a reading teacher, I knew that reading to a child was a meaningful way to kick-start their own reading journey. So, to get him interested in my favorite children's book, *The Hobbit*, I brought in some *Hobbit* Legos® to get the ball rolling, Middle Earth-wise. Did I use Legos® to coerce a seven-year-old into opening a book? Why, yes. Yes, I did.

Then one day, I casually asked if he'd like to read *The Hobbit* together. Henry promptly replied, "No."

So I dropped my voice down an octave into my best movie-trailer imitation and said, "Are you sure? It's a book about a world with wizards and dwarves who go on an epic quest to reclaim their homeland and rescue a pile of stolen gold from a fire-breathing dragon. Would you like to read a book all about that?"

I'm happy to report that Henry enthusiastically agreed to reading a story like that. For thirty minutes a week over the next couple of years, I read *The Hobbit* out loud to him. I performed my best wizard, dragon, dwarf, and hobbit voices for him. I sang the song lyrics from the book as best I could. We took a week off here and there to work on homework or play sports outside, but we always returned to the book.

By the time fifth grade came around, Henry not only scored at the highest reading comprehension level on the state test but was also recognized in front of his class as the best reader in his class.

At the end of that year, Henry had to write a short paper about a reliable friend in his life. Henry chose to write about me and how I introduced him to his favorite book, *The Hobbit*. Just as the stories of friends on a television show reminded the world that we weren't as alone as we may have felt, a fictional and fantastical tale on the pages of a book created a refuge where Henry and I learned to trust that enduring difficult times together is worth the effort. When Henry went on to junior high, I followed him there, meeting with him every week, playing basketball, playing checkers, helping with homework, watching him grow to earn As and play three sports. I was and am so proud of the person he became and all the obstacles he overcame to get there.

I am also proud and grateful that I played a small part in helping Henry through his difficult early start in life. But the truth is, Henry helped me more than he knew when he let me share my love of Middle Earth with him, shot baskets with me, schooled me in UNO, and offered me his friendship in thirty-minute deposits every week. The afternoons I spent at his schools gave me a place to rest from the challenges I faced at work and in my personal life. When I drove to his campus, week after week, year after year, I often felt nearer to the heart of God than at any other time. There was a kind of salvation and rest in mentoring Henry because his need for friendship after his father's passing pulled me out of my selfish, small world.

Mentoring taught me that work and rest often go hand in hand when the work involves friendship. Some weeks, when I arrived worn down and weary with my cares, simply working to help someone who could do nothing back for me helped me find a kind of rest in the heart of God I could not find any other way.

Jesus reinforced this idea in Matthew 11 when he promised us that his kind of work (or yoke) provides rest for anyone who has been worn down:

> Come to me, all you who are weary and burdened, and I will give you rest. Take my yoke upon you and learn from me, for I am gentle and humble in heart, and you will find rest for your souls. For my yoke is easy and my burden is light. (Matt. 11:28–30 NIV)

What Jesus knows, and what I learned from befriending a first grader whose life was vastly different from mine, is that at its core, the yoke of Christ requires self-giving. When we pay the cost of loving and serving others, we ensure we don't miss out on the *manoach* rest Jesus offers.

Perhaps, when we reach for 57.1 billion minutes of relational comfort to remind us that life won't always be so heavy and hard, what we want is the light and easy yoke Christ offers anyone who will come to him instead of staring at a screen. When things go south, when a pandemic hits and we're quarantined, when we have a friend we wish could become more than a friend, when we have a roommate who hates us, when we meet a kid facing impossible odds, we can turn to our divine friend for even better wisdom than Naomi offered Ruth.

After all, Jesus risked like none other to bring us into a rest like none other, the rest only the gospel can offer.

STORIES
from our FRIENDS

Joy through the Ups and Downs of Life

BY LEAH

"Can I borrow twenty dollars?" was the question Tim asked each time he saw me. Tim, you see, was homeless. And I was a volunteer with the homeless ministry at Mosaic Church.

I politely declined every time until finally, I responded like this: "Tim, I will never give you money. But I will give you something more valuable than money. And that is my friendship."

In the beginning, I had a goal to "fix" Tim. I was determined to solve his problems and get him off the streets. I spent countless hours driving him to medical appointments. I bought him a phone and put him on my family plan so we could keep in touch. That worked well until I discovered he was a drug dealer. "Tim, I can't pay for your cell phone anymore," I said. But we remained friends. I discovered he had killed two people in his past. Instead of rejecting him, I made his favorite tuna sandwiches every Sunday. His life was unpredictable and unstable and sometimes downright dangerous. Through it all, he learned to trust me and know he could count on me, no matter what.

We had one fight. He failed to keep an appointment with me. "I'm out of town," he said.

"No, you're not!" I yelled. "I'm standing here looking at you under the bridge!!!" He later apologized for lying to me.

And I forgave him. He smiles a bit sheepishly about that one fight, and we both laugh.

Tim loved coming to my house. He took long, hot showers and then donned a bathing suit. He sat in the backyard by the pool, smoked a cigarette, and thought deep thoughts while I washed his clothes. He relaxed and occasionally fell asleep on the couch. I would cover him with a soft blanket and enjoy the peaceful look on his face.

One year, I put a photo of Tim on our family Christmas card. I framed the card for him. He carried it in his backpack, everywhere he went, for about two years. We were no longer just friends; we were now family.

We have weathered arrests, jail pickups, health crises, addictions, and countless other experiences together.

"Wow, you're such a great person for loving a guy like that," some say. But the truth is this: Tim brings as much or more to my life than I do to his. He has given me gifts of jewelry (hopefully not stolen) and flowers (dug from a dumpster). He sends beautiful cards, handcrafted for me from jailhouse artists. He tells me to "take what I need" from his bank account, because he is extremely generous.

"I've got your back," he assures me, because he wants to protect me.

"Friends love through all kinds of weather, and families stick together in all kinds of trouble" (Prov. 17:17 *The Message*). I love Tim through the ups and downs of his life, and he loves me through the ups and downs of mine. And we are both richer for it.

Chapter 8

THE POWER OF REDEMPTION

I Will Do All You Ask

"And now, my daughter, don't be afraid. I will do for you all you ask."

—Ruth 3:11 NIV

I n a brilliant scene from the classically quotable 1987 fairy-tale movie *The Princess Bride*,[1] a group of plucky heroes set out on a quest. This beleaguered band of brothers headed to a castle to rescue a princess and enact justice for a crime committed by a wicked prince. Unfortunately, they were a bit shorthanded, and their best warrior, the mysterious "Man in Black," had been tortured into unconsciousness by that evil prince. To revive the "Man in Black" and even the odds, our heroes carried the barely breathing body of their friend to a healer in the forest named Miracle Max (played by the clearly-having-a-good-time Billy Crystal).

Miracle Max and his wife, Valerie, concocted a miracle pill, coated it in chocolate (to make it go down easier, naturally), and

---

[1] *The Princess Bride*, directed by Rob Reiner (Los Angeles: 20th Century Fox, 1987).

force-fed it to the "Man in Black." The group of heroes, full of hope in the power of the pill, raced off, dragging their unconscious friend behind them. Max called out as they left his forest cottage, "Have fun storming the castle!"

Under her breath, Valerie whispered to Max, "Do you think it will work?"

Waving and smiling at the men, Max muttered to her, "It would take a miracle."

These heroes in this scene offer us a picture of any great kingdom work and all great gospel friendships. We spend our lives "storming the castle," doing the work we feel called to do on our way toward a (hopefully) better, more redeemed future. We carry high hopes and injured friends as we cling to a mission larger than ourselves. The tricky reality we try not to mutter too much about is that our efforts and friendships often require a miracle to survive.

In Ruth 3, we find another plucky group of multiethnic, multigenerational friends—Ruth and Naomi—in a similar place. They, too, needed a miracle.

At Naomi's counsel, our protagonist, Ruth, dressed up and arrived at Boaz's business late at night, where she hoped he could be her Miracle Max. Ruth's actions may seem like forward and "modern" behavior for ancient women, but Ruth had good cause to show up with this hope in her heart. Boaz, a refined and wealthy man, clearly favored Ruth. More crucially, as Naomi hinted at the end of chapter 2, she, Ruth, and Boaz shared a unique familial connection. When Ruth returned home from gleaning and shared all that happened in Boaz's field, Naomi couldn't believe her stroke of luck (what we have seen is God's hidden hand) and exclaimed: "That man is our close relative; he is one of our guardian-redeemers" (Ruth 2:20 NIV).

Let's take a moment to unpack the revelation of this crucial plot detail. What, exactly, was a "guardian-redeemer," or what some translations call a "kinsman-redeemer"?

In the book of Leviticus, God established the Year of Jubilee to restrain the pervasiveness of poverty in the land. Every fifty years, in the Year of Jubilee, any land sold by an impoverished family was returned to that family's male heir (Lev. 25:23–28). So, Naomi knew Elimelech's land could be returned to his descendants someday. However, that year was not the Year of Jubilee, and Elimelech had no male heirs. Thankfully, the law made provisions that allowed the redemption of an impoverished family's land in non-Jubilee years, even if they had no apparent heirs.

This secondary provision allowed for the family to find a guardian-redeemer or, in Hebrew, a *go-el*. A *go-el* was a distant relative of the impoverished family who acted as a ransomer and redeemer by buying back the family land and ensuring the broken family's future. Hope dawned in Naomi when she realized Boaz was their distant relative with enough wealth to buy back their land as their *go-el*. But would he do it? Because becoming a *go-el* required more than anteing up financially.

Not only would Boaz have to spend his fortune to buy the land for Naomi's family, but he would also have to marry a widow in the family, and their children would be considered Elimelech's heirs, not Boaz's. As the *go-el*, Boaz would relinquish his right to continue his family line and legacy, and all his fortune would pass into another man's lineage. He would be reigniting a dead man's estate by marrying and having a son through the deceased's widow.

Elimelech's family contained only two widows, and neither seemed entirely appealing from a cultural standpoint. Naomi was past childbearing age and couldn't produce an heir. Ruth was a

Moabitess, an outsider, and (mostly) a foreigner to his faith. Would Boaz, a faithful Jewish man, be willing to marry Ruth?

It would take a miracle.

Naomi did some quick math, added up Boaz's favor toward Ruth plus his seeming heart for redemption, and the women gave it their best shot. Ruth found Boaz asleep after a long day of work, laid down at his feet, and when he awoke, she said to him, "Spread the corner of your garment over me, since you are a guardian-redeemer" (Ruth 3:9 NIV).

In those days, Ruth's actions communicated one explicit request: *Marry me. Put a ring on it, Boaz.*

Ruth asked Boaz to cover her and Naomi with his wealth, power, and authority to redeem their family. What would Boaz say? Would he reject her? Would Boaz call her crazy or accuse her of gold-digging? Would he respond angrily, balking at the prospect of relinquishing his family name or marrying a foreigner like her? If Ruth feared any of this, Boaz's kind response put all her fears to rest when he said, "I will do for you all you ask" (Ruth 3:11 NIV).

Ruth proposed, and Boaz said yes. Eventually, he paid her debt and took her to be his wife. After that, all his wealth and status, which she neither earned through birthright nor worked directly to achieve, legally and automatically, became hers and Naomi's. Forever.

There's your miracle.

True redemption always requires one.

MORGAN

Have Fun Storming the Building

Churches, like friendships, can fall on hard times for many reasons. Churches, like families, have ups and downs.

The church where I now serve as lead pastor was experiencing its own relentless set of "downs" a number of years ago. A series of decisions by previous leadership had left the church shrinking and gasping for breath. No one was willing or able to serve as lead pastor, so Carrie and I were asked to move back from Nashville to fill that role.

Once we arrived, the congregation, which had once included approximately six hundred people, had bottomed out to roughly 150. The massive budget cuts had necessitated corresponding reductions in staffing. The loss of staff resulted in more congregants leaving, which meant more financial resources departed with them. The people who remained hoped for brighter days, but the death spiral of the previous few years had left them drained. Effectively, when I became lead pastor in 2009, Mosaic resembled a new church plant with the unusual bonuses of a mortgage and a traumatic past.

That pesky mortgage was a doozy. Sometimes, people debate the goodness or badness of churches owning buildings, facilities, or property. Certainly, around the topic of real estate and all its trappings lies a tension we must grapple with as leaders and pastors. As a campus missionary for more than a dozen years, focusing on universities across the country, I understand that the kingdom of God is, and must be, much more than an organization occupying brick-and-mortar spaces. Twice in my life, I've been a member of church plants that required the tedious weekly task of setting up and tearing down chairs and equipment. It was a worthy but costly sacrifice. After experiencing church with and without a building, I suppose you could say I have landed in the place where I like for the speakers to stay where we hang them and the chairs to stay where we put them so all the people can put their time into other sacrificial endeavors. Without question, though, if a church forgets it is also for the community and not just for itself, the building can become a polarizing reminder of mission drift or forgetfulness.

Regardless, in our case, the facility was perhaps the remaining physical driver holding that band of brothers and sisters together. Just as a house or apartment offers space where our lives take shape and build relationships, a building gives a church family a space to be shaped and built together into a community capable of loving well. However, holding our key physical driver in place was one key financial giver. At that time, Mosaic had one extraordinarily generous family who had remained through the chaos of the leadership transition and happened to give a third of our budget every month. Without their monthly five-figure offering, our remaining slashed budget—even as bare bones and don't-use-the-heat-in-winter as it was—would have been impossible to maintain.

But then, after serving only a few months as lead pastor, that man and his family decided they weren't connecting with me or our church's new vision, and they left to find another church. While I understood they needed to go and harbored no hard feelings toward them, this news terrified me.

It's easy, in hindsight, to feel only gratitude for them because of the blessing they were to Mosaic for so long. But I will never forget where I was or what it felt like to answer the phone and hear the news he was leaving and that Mosaic faced a dead-end cliff over a pit of financial death. Tens and tens of thousands of dollars cannot just be conjured up every month. That kind of cash does not exist between the sofa cushions in the church nursery, nor is it stuffed in an electrical closet somewhere—trust me, I've looked. Mosaic still had no savings and no way to pay our bills. Our options were to fire the remaining four staff (including me) or sell the building, and both seemed tantamount to organizational suicide after all the congregation had gone through. What could we do? We were trying to storm the castle, but the weight of a barely breathing budget kept getting heavier.

My friend John, a neonatologist and one of our new elders, took command of the situation and my fearful pastor's heart and said, "Get the staff, go to the church, we're going to pray!"

We gathered to pray in a little abandoned overflow room next to the main worship room. The aesthetic of the room told the story of the strain of our budget with its moldy carpet (water kept leaking in from the outside), stained ceiling tiles (no money to replace them), cheap plastic tables, and some folding chairs. We kept the doors to that embarrassingly gross room shut on Sundays as people walked past it and used air purifiers to keep down the gag-inducing smell.

A desperately bedraggled room seemed like an appropriate place for some plucky castle stormers to pray for a miracle. We prayed things like, "God, we need you. God, if you don't come through, we are done. We are trusting in you and you alone." Looking back, it occurs to me now that we could have quoted Ruth and asked God to spread the corner of his garment over us. We needed so much from him that we could never do for ourselves. We read the Bible, rebuked our fear, claimed God's abundant provision, cast out any enemy keeping us from finding a way through, and declared God's goodness and might for as long as we could. Then we went home and waited for whatever would come next.

In the meantime, I had to stand in the pulpit for the next few Sundays, look the congregation in the eye, and pretend nothing was wrong. I knew we might not have a building next month, but until that was a verifiable fact, I had to act like everything was superbly excellent. As I played games with my four young children, I imagined explaining the worst news to them. We had moved them away from their Nashville friends only a few months before to try to rescue this "princess bride," this precious part of the bride of Christ. What if it hadn't worked? How would I tell them our miracle didn't happen?

Here, where my desperation peaked and God's silence seemed deafening, is where the story gets good. Behind our main parking lot, Mosaic owned a smaller building. This fateful Building C had been untouched since 1975, and its interior made our gross little overflow room in the main building look like the Taj Mahal. Walking into Building C was like walking into a moldy, creepy, broken-down time capsule. We had listed it for sale or rent months before, but once tenants saw the photos, they passed on gutting and retrofitting the old building.

But within thirty days of that desperate prayer meeting in the moldy room, we received a call from an interested potential tenant. By the way, you only need one call when you have the greatest miracle worker in the universe in your corner. Our one call came from a company who wanted to rent Building C for—wait for it—the exact amount, dollar for dollar, every month we lost when our generous giver moved on. That business signed a five-year lease, which gave our church a new figurative lease on life and running room to grow. Coincidentally (or not), we signed that rental contract in the little overflow room where we had the original prayer meeting.

In one sense, every good thing that has happened through Mosaic has happened because of that one miracle moment of resurrection and revival. What we couldn't do for ourselves, God did for us. When we couldn't see a path forward, God carved one out of an impossible dead end. When we were mostly dead, God carried us, revived us, and redeemed us. I like to think that, as Valerie said in *The Princess Bride*, God had fun storming the castle (or gross old building) for us.

Isn't this always the way salvation works? Eventually, every church, person, relationship, and friendship will face a moment in which, unless God comes and supernaturally provides, moving forward will not be possible. It always takes a redemptive miracle to make it in the kingdom of God because, as Ephesians 2:9 says, God saves us by grace and "not by works, so that no one can boast"(NIV). Ruth and Naomi received a redemptive miracle when Boaz said yes. Just as redemptive grace makes us new creations in Christ (2 Cor. 5:17), the redemptive miracle Boaz gave them birthed Ruth and Naomi into entirely new lives.

What kind of redemptive miracles can we expect to see in our friendships?

CARRIE

New Friends, Old Wounds

A number of years ago, some leaders in our church family operated in unhealthy and even cruel ways. Many of those leaders left the church once a few brave people exposed their abusive leadership behavior and choices. Some stayed, though. They went to counseling, repented to the people they had hurt, and forfeited their positions of authority and influence. But one day, I saw one of those leaders sitting in the back of the room, which triggered my anger and fear about the past. All kinds of questions surfaced as a result. How do we continue to love people who have hurt us? How can we trust someone who proved untrustworthy in the past? I questioned whether this leader should be allowed to remain in the community with the people he failed. Then a horrific question arose in my mind: Would he be allowed to lead again someday? Surely not! I approached our friend Kevin, a trusted mentor and incredible organizational leader, for help with some of my questions. In truth, I secretly longed to hear Kevin validate my feelings of resentment and promise that a leader who had failed should never, ever be allowed to have any authority ever again.

Kevin walked me through a brief history of how various churches and ministries have handled leadership failures throughout the twentieth century. He validated my questions and explained how other spiritual families and organizations had chosen to answer similar questions. Then he pointed out that the leader I struggled to forgive and trust had no current authority and might never be restored to any place of influence. Kevin paused then and said something that has shaped me as a Christian: "But I hope he can be. Because at some point, we are either people who believe in redemption and reconciliation, or we aren't."

Kevin's words acted like a kind of defibrillator for my spiritual heart, causing it to beat for redemption in a way I hadn't previously experienced. Like Kevin, I started to long to see the failed and broken people who wounded me restored and flourishing in God's grace. I still believed leaders should be held accountable for their harmful actions, but a new banner of hope waved above the interventions and confrontations I witnessed. The drumbeat of my heart insisted that while history had formed the circumstances of today, God's redemptive power could shape our future.

The man I once thought I couldn't forgive is now a dear, trusted friend to Morgan and me. He has flourished, and God has restored him in beautiful ways. Our once-painful friendship that inspired my many questions taught me how our friendships hold power to heal old wounds. I'm grateful for that lesson because, since then, a few of my own failures have proven I am equally in need of friends who can believe I'm worthy of redemption, too.

New Wounds, Old Friends

One night a few years after my conversation with Kevin, I chattered away at a dinner party with some friends, and I suddenly realized I had said something . . . wrong. A strange look passed over my old friend's face when the words escaped my mouth, and

I knew I had messed up. But even though I could sense his pain, I didn't understand how my words caused it. Given that none of the White people at the table seemed to notice but all the Black people's eyebrows rose, I was clued into the kind of offense I had committed. I began to literally sweat as the conversation kept going. I didn't intend to hurt my friend, but that wasn't the point. A heart that beats for redemption will bear the responsibility to heal the damage our words or actions inflict. The only thing worse than facing the consequences of my mistake or ignorance would be to shirk my responsibility for my actions and then endlessly repeat that mistake.

Later, when I could speak privately with my friend, he explained why my words held so much power to wound him. Those words had bound me up with people who had harmed him with racist actions and words. Tears filled my eyes as I apologized and asked him to forgive me. I wanted to be someone who spoke life and love, but I had failed miserably. My dear, wonderful friend and I journeyed through that painful conversation together, and he graciously gave me space to grow and learn how to be a better friend. I am forever grateful.

New Friends, New Mercies

Many years later, that lesson about the power of words came to me again through another friend, Johanna. Johanna is Chinese American, and she has taught me a great deal about the racism many Asian Americans experience in their day-to-day lives in the United States—and in Austin.

Austin is a city full of new growth and tech company transplants, and it has few local natives. When you meet someone new, the first question most people here will ask is, "Are you from Austin?" and since the usual answer is no, the follow-up question is always, "Where are you from?" Johanna shared one night that sometimes, when she tells people she's from Chicago, they ask, "But, where are you *really* from?" Some people even then compliment her English and express amazement that she sounds like an American.

Johanna is "really" from Chicago. As in, she was born and bred in Chi-Town. Johanna is the person I will ask for restaurant recommendations and advice when and if I ever get to visit the Windy City. She and her husband, Jeremy, the world's biggest Chicago sports fan, order the famous Giordano's pizza in the mail so they can eat authentic Chicago pizza in Austin. Johanna has the most adorable faint Chicagoan accent. You absolutely, 100 percent, could never accidentally get the impression from a chat with Johanna that she is not actually from Chicago but secretly hides some other tale of origin. Except that was what was happening to her regularly here in Texas.

Please allow me to insist we stop making these kinds of comments to Asian Americans. Because first of all, this unabashed nosiness is rude. Why strangers feel they have the right to ask probing, clarifying questions in the middle of small talk at the park is beyond comprehension. Second, by asking someone where they are "really" from or congratulating them on their American accent (when they just told you they are from the United States!), the implication is that they are an outsider.

A few years ago, when Johanna was still fairly new to Mosaic, she shared at a church gathering about a recent incident involving a White classmate bullying her daughter at school with insensitive, racist comments. My heart ached as I internally lamented the reality that people who look like me regularly treated Johanna and her family like people who don't belong. I opened my mouth and said the only thing I could think to say: "I want to apologize for all the hurt that people who look like me have caused in your life. I hope

Mosaic can be a place where you feel safe and experience people honoring you and loving you for who you are."

Just as I once hadn't understood the power of my words to wound, I didn't anticipate my words would help Johanna as they did. When she and I recently reminisced about that conversation, Johanna shared that over the years, she often felt pressured in church settings to prove she was American. My apology made space for her to be authentic with nothing to prove.

While we may wound and bless others unintentionally in every relationship in our lives, intentionally humble, vulnerable, and kind words are critical in redemptive friendships. When our friend John said, "We're going to pray," when the friend I wounded said, "We need to talk," when Johanna said, "I'd like to share something," when I said, "I'm sorry," and when Boaz said, "I will do all you ask," those words revealed hearts that beat for redemption.

Hearts that beat for redemption long for more than allowing people to glean scraps of grain for mere survival. Hearts that beat for redemption say words such as, *I will pay the price to see your broken life made whole. I will empty my heart and my house and risk all I have to see you made whole because I can't be healed and whole until you are healed and whole.* Ultimately, hearts that beat for redemption just expect that friendships come with unanticipated price tags.

Boaz and the Other Guy

Although Boaz affirmed his willingness to pay the cost of Ruth's redemption, he noted another family member who was closer to Naomi's family, which introduces a new tension into the story:

> Although it is true that I am a guardian-redeemer of
> our family, there is another who is more closely related
> than I. Stay here for the night, and in the morning if he

> wants to do his duty as your guardian-redeemer, good;
> let him redeem you. But if he is not willing, as surely as
> the LORD lives I will do it. (Ruth 3:12–13 NIV)

In Ruth 4, the other potential *go-el* could have paid the cost to redeem Ruth, but when he realized marrying Ruth as a *go-el* would endanger his own estate, he more or less said, *I won't do it. I can't do it. It's too costly.* Why would he say this? Why would his heart not beat to redeem?

It was clear: marrying Ruth would have cost him his cultural value of a legacy founded on financial and family success. Similarly, diverse friendships sometimes ask us to relinquish our loyalty to cultural values and priorities, which can feel like losing parts of our identity. When Boaz lost his right to give his descendants his name, the most significant marker of success in that culture, we witness a faithfulness to redemption that points us toward Christ. The Bible often uses marriage metaphors to explain the relationship of God with his people, and we find this metaphor mirrored in Boaz's Christlike sacrifice for Ruth's redemption. In his culture, people married for status, security, and stability. What could motivate Boaz to give up his social status, financial security, and stability for Ruth?

Simply put, he loved her. In a world where love rarely preceded marriage, Boaz agreed to give up as much as necessary for the sake of love:

> "The LORD bless you, my daughter," he replied. "This
> kindness is greater than that which you showed earlier:
> You have not run after the younger men, whether rich
> or poor. And now, my daughter, don't be afraid. I will do
> for you all you ask. All the people of my town know that
> you are a woman of noble character." (Ruth 3:10–11 NIV)

Love motivates people to do seemingly crazy things and pay costs they never expected. Married people experience the cost of love in various ways through their relationship. In marriage, the two become one (Gen. 2:24), which means that in marriage, we must learn to equally honor and carry two unique life experiences, two distinct perspectives, and two family histories as we pledge ourselves daily to one shared love. People who have married someone of different ability, culture, race, or socioeconomic background experience the cost of this vow in even more distinct and concentrated doses. Somehow, long before the Messiah came to redeem humanity from our sin, Boaz understood that sacrificial love and redemption went hand in hand. We prove we know that, too, when we hold up the willingness of a divine groom to give himself wholly to us despite how different we are from him in every way.

Jesus is the truer and better Boaz, who shaped history through the power of his redemptive heart and endured the cost required to redeem the lives of people unlike him. Boaz gave up his name so he could share a life with Ruth, but Jesus gave his life so we could share his name for eternity. In Jesus, who has loved us infinitely more than even Boaz loved Ruth, we find the power to carry us through struggles, failures, and conflicts.

Multiethnic, multigenerational, and socioeconomically diverse relationships are costly. Sometimes they can feel like they are costing us everything. They cost us swallowing our tongue, forgiving over and over, being willing to listen and learn new things and humble ourselves repeatedly—sometimes to remain in a relationship with people who may not deserve our love or our loyalty. But in the end, these kinds of relationships are priceless because they give us a front-row view of the kind of miracle only God's grace can accomplish.

And that's when the fun part of storming the castle begins. Miracle Max would undoubtedly approve.

STORIES
from our FRIENDS

Attending to Justice

BY MEAGAN HARDING

I grew up in a small Black Baptist church with my dad as my pastor. I spent many summers going to revivals in wooden churches filled with reverent, joyous, and generous "melanated" saints. Those saints shaped me, and they carry me still. My understanding of what it meant to love people well, care for my community, and pursue justice came from my parents' example and those red-padded pews. My faith community was my refuge.

When Michael Brown was killed in Ferguson, Missouri, I was ripped apart. I was hurt, angry, and already tired. The calls for peace and unity came swiftly, but the demands for justice were siloed and often only came from those who looked like me. The public expressions of lament as I scrolled on my social media timelines were from those who could see ourselves in him. Michael Brown was killed on a Saturday, and church was the next day, but it didn't feel like I would be walking into a refuge. Just out of college and attending Mosaic, I started to ask hard questions to my church leadership and White members.

Questions like if you love me (so many swore they did), then why do you say nothing when people who look like me are murdered unjustly? Have you ever thought that voting motivated by a single issue supports policies and people that undermine equality? On a lighter note, why doesn't the worship, with diverse faces on stage, actually reflect different cultures instead of only singing contemporary Christian music songs? Why don't we make space to lament? What are you willing to pay for this unity you keep saying you want?

See, if diversity is expressed only for its own sake, it can often be harmful to people who have been marginalized. It often reinforces them as "other" while asking so little of nonmarginalized, often White, people. However, diversity is helpful in illuminating our blind spots and exposing our biases. It helps us break out of echo chambers and challenges our views of what it means to have a just society. Creating a space for belonging often starts with the deconstruction of what is "normal."

But we don't just get there by only singing together on Sundays or enjoying small groups together. It must be pursued through intention by auditing how we spend our money, what policies we support, how we use our voices in our places of influence, and how we commit to our own learning and unlearning. The root of my questions (and what I was really asking the White people with whom I worshiped and who said they loved me) was: *How will you show up for me? How deep does your love go? How will you lay down your life for me?*

Many people at Mosaic began the painful and laborious work of interrogating their own prejudices and biases. They showed up time and time again with lament and questions of their own after self-study. They admitted what they didn't know and searched for answers. They made space for my anger, pain, and confusion. And they let me challenge their beliefs about how the world works for everyone, spurring them toward a new understanding and letting Jesus rework their perspective. It was and is messy. It was and is necessary. It was and is healing. It was and is the work of the gospel. Justice doesn't just happen. The Bible says to "pursue justice" or "seek justice," meaning it must be attended to. If Christians want a unified country and world, then we will have to get real about sacrificial love, which means, frankly, those in the majority must lay down their lives and emulate those seasoned Black saints who raised me and who knew that there was no freedom without sacrifice.

Chapter 9

BOAZ'S CHOICE

Leaning into the Present

Then Boaz announced to the elders and all the people, "Today you are witnesses."

—Ruth 4:9 NIV

Even though we're already discussing how Naomi and Ruth's story intersects the uncomfortable topics of racism, ageism, and classism, a proper consideration of the text also asks us to consider our relationships and how they're affected by political ideologies and affiliations. Take a deep breath and buckle in, because Ruth's lessons about navigating a difficult political landscape may help shed some light upon the dark path of our era, one marked by tribalism and deep polarization.

After all, the book begins by reminding us that it occurs in the time of the judges (the *shoftim*), a time when Israel had no king or centralized political authority and when everyone did whatever seemed right to them (Judg. 21:25). Judges ends with a shocking and brutal protest against injustice that rocked the nation. A lack of secure borders during that time likely contributed to the fluidity

169

of Elimelech's immigration. And, while the story of Ruth doesn't carry overt messages about political theory, its political landscape does impact its story arc.

The book of Ruth tells the plight of two refugees arriving from an enemy nation who must rely on a society's ability to enforce its moral and ethical laws to help them survive. It's also the story about the family of a future favorite political king, who would one day rule and reign for forty years. While Ruth may not argue for one political party or another, it does remind us that we aren't the first people to live through a time of political instability and protests. We aren't the first people facing the complications of poverty, refugees, and the insecurity of societal consequences produced by the unreliability of people's choices and beliefs.

To put it more succinctly, the book of Ruth has something to say about how political diversity is handled within a community. Let's begin in Ruth 4 and marvel at the choices Boaz made in a time when he could have chosen to do whatever suited him best.

Choosing Love and Law

As Ruth 4 opens, we find Boaz navigating a sticky situation at the town gate. After Ruth offered herself to him and proposed marriage by his bed in the middle of the night, Boaz nonetheless chose not to engage sexually with her before marriage. Nor did he decide to disregard the legal obligations of being a *go-el*. Boaz's choice to pull together love (say yes to a marriage that would cost him his name) and law (honor God's Word with respect to sexual ethics) in Ruth 4 reveals an important principle about how we interact with one another and with the rules of our society.

Boaz could have chosen differently and found a way to justify the decision. His internal logic could have insisted that sex with Ruth was perfectly defensible. After all, she dressed up, put on her perfume, laid down at his feet, and appeared to consent to whatever he wished. He could have felt he deserved the right to enjoy a night of passion with this woman he had provided for and protected in his fields. Or, Boaz could have taken a split-the-hairs-and-look-for-the-loophole stance and done only part of what Ruth asked. Ruth asked him to redeem their family, which by law would require him to buy back Elimelech's land and marry Ruth. He could have done only part of that. Or further still, Boaz could have slept with Ruth and married her but refused to repurchase Elimelech's land and restore his family line.

But Boaz did not seek to justify a decision that benefited himself most of all. Between the lines of Ruth 4, we see Boaz's heart softening toward Ruth's plight and pain. Even as we sense his attraction for Ruth increasing, Boaz honored the law of God, which reserved sexual relationships for marital unions between one man and one woman for life (Lev. 18). He obeyed both Leviticus 19:34, which asked him to love the foreigner, and Leviticus 25:25, when he sacrificed to restore the impoverished line of his family. Boaz also honored God's call to love God as Deuteronomy 6:5 commanded and obeyed Leviticus 19:18 by loving his neighbor as himself.

Boaz honored God's law and love when he denied himself the right to do as he pleased, either way. He understood that God doesn't care solely about the biblical / God-honoring ends of a story (where we often land). God also cares about the biblical / God-honoring means that get us to that ending. We can't betray in a moment what God says is good and automatically expect to achieve or become something good in the end. Ethics matter because God's law matters, and God's law matters because ethics matter.

Boaz then went to the public square in daylight, at the city gate, where all kinds of eyes were all up in his business because he understood that his personal, individual choices carried public, collective weight. He involved the town elders, Naomi's relatives, and anyone cruising the main drag in Bethlehem in that business:

> Meanwhile Boaz went up to the town gate and sat down there just as the guardian-redeemer he had mentioned came along. Boaz said, "Come over here, my friend, and sit down." So he went over and sat down.
>
> Boaz took ten of the elders of the town and said, "Sit here," and they did so. Then he said to the guardian-redeemer, "Naomi, who has come back from Moab, is selling the piece of land that belonged to our relative Elimelek. I thought I should bring the matter to your attention and suggest that you buy it in the presence of these seated here and in the presence of the elders of my people." (Ruth 4:1–4 NIV)

Boaz honored the law of God and revealed his intentions for three reasons:

1. This public conversation allowed Boaz to keep his promise to do all Ruth asked of him.
2. It honored his family duty by offering the other man to potentially claim his right to act as the *go-el*.
3. It showed reverence for God, who expected Boaz to love well and act justly.

Boaz was not an old-fashioned guy flaunting his self-control regarding sexual morality. Neither was he a modern-day activist demanding a complete justice-centered overhaul of the lives of everyone present at the city gates. Instead of making a deal in the dark with Ruth, he led into the light with an incredible blend of law and love.

In our modern era, we rarely find law and love blended in this same way when political discussions become heated between

Christians. We tend to prioritize one or the other when it comes to viewpoints and convictions. Let's look at a cautionary tale that highlights the pain often caused by the difficulties around political differences in our friendships.

MORGAN

Politics in the Pews

I recently had a conversation with someone leaving Mosaic, who cited a familiar narrative regarding their decision to end their active participation in our congregation. The conversation went like this:

"Morgan, I'm leaving because my politics aren't accepted here."

I asked for a more in-depth explanation of how they had arrived at this conclusion.

"Whenever I say certain things, sometimes people give me pushback."

I then spoke of one of my great hopes, that our church would be a community where, on the one hand, everyone feels warmly accepted. Still, on the other, we might experience some occasional, justified pushback from someone with a different perspective; this is, after all, how we often grow. Our parents push back on us, our spouses push back on us, our teachers and coaches push back on us with the goal of betterment; surely this might happen from fellow Christians as well.

With this in mind, I then asked them to imagine if someone from what they perceive to be the "other side" of an issue said something they believe to be potentially non-Christian or false. If that were to happen, I suggested, perhaps they might want that person also to experience pushback. I pointed to how conflicting perspectives are inherent in all relational spaces, but those conflicts heighten in diverse relationships.

Sometimes, this line of reasoning helps the person who has felt disrespected or marginalized to find a new footing and reason to stay. When this is the case, the person often develops a reinvigorated passion for finding common ground, believes the best about the people with opposing views in new ways, and sees added benefits to living in communion with people they don't always agree with regarding hot topics.

However, this most recent conversation did not end that way.

"Well, I guess that's all true," they said. "But I really can't stay. I don't feel like there's space for my political beliefs, and I just want to go to a church where people agree with me."

"So, are the politics of the people in your church more important to you than the congregation's beliefs about the person of Christ, the Bible, the gospel, and the love we are called to express to one another?" I asked.

"Well, no . . ." his voice trailed off. "But I'm just exhausted."

My heart dropped at this point because I had to tell someone I love and care for that I would deeply miss them, as would our whole community. This person was genuinely surprised when I shared that people from the "other side" also often left feeling exhausted for the same reasons. The truth is that weary or offended people from any "side" can feel unsupported and excluded in a diverse church. Those feelings result in a loss of connection to the greater sense of belonging we all seek in our spiritual families. That loss of connection can lead to accusations against the pastoral team and church leadership. Left-leaning members usually accuse us of "letting them down," while right-leaning members insist we have led in "unbiblical ways."

These responses highlight an important distinction about how our modern political ideologies intersect with our church expectations. While the relational loss breaks my heart as a friend and as a pastor, it also leaves me wrestling with how to lead in a way that fosters a prioritization of relational honor while making space for different political beliefs. As a Christian pastor with distinct, passionate political views, I can sympathize with people who decide to leave our church over political conflict. Sociable interaction with people politically unlike me is uncomfortable and sometimes infuriating. Learning to make space for other viewpoints is an arduous task. The sad reality we face as modern Christians is that it's often easier to stomach the discomfort of ethnic or socioeconomic diversity than the conflicts created by our political diversity. Our political discomfort begs us to reach for an answer to one question in particular: How can we embrace one another amid political diversity?

Certainly not all choices and beliefs can be considered equally good, righteous, godly, or defensible. And not all opinions should be tolerated, especially when those beliefs produce practices or policies that are discriminatory, harmful, or blatantly non-Christian in some way. When we read about debates over political decisions made a hundred or more years ago, the best answers often seem so obvious. Jesus spoke to this truth when he said in Luke 7:35 that "wisdom is proved right by all her children" (NIV). Hindsight allows the privilege of an unemotional perspective and a list of all the positive or negative effects of a policy or political viewpoint. Concerning our current debates and disagreements, we have only our education, experiences, gut feelings, and best guesses about the future.

When your best guess and my best guess are at odds, when we both point to biblical evidence that we believe supports our viewpoint, and when the irreconcilability of our discussion threatens to break our bond of friendship, how can blending law and love show us a way forward together?

A (Politically) Blended Family

In our relational conflicts involving our political preferences, clashes intensify when we fill our lives with more of God's law or more of God's love, to the detriment of the other. For conservative-leaning people, we often flood our minds, conversations, and social media feeds with the law (or our version of it). We believe in things like "law and order" (and not just the television show). On our darker days, we assume our ability to live a morally good life will save us from all kinds of earthly and eternal suffering. We might even expect our perfect record to let us off the hook from being expected to ensure our neighbors' well-being. After all, the dark side of moralism tells us that if everyone followed the same rules and played the game how we played it, they wouldn't have problems we haven't personally experienced. Mercy is a good antidote when our limited human perspective silences God's voice of compassion toward others.

For liberal-leaning people, we often flood our minds, conversations, and feeds with the love of God (or our version of it). The ethical waters muddy quite a bit for us when we begin to believe our ability to love our neighbors alone can save us from the dark side of our humanity. We then feel little to no obligation to bend our knees to a God who establishes moral standards and expects his people to obey them. Pondering how rules and laws maintain justice *and* require acts of mercy is good medicine for us when our hearts fear God's boundaries will exclude someone unjustly.

I'm not sure to what extent Boaz was tempted to abandon either the love or the law of God, but incredibly, he honored both. Perhaps, on the night he promised to do all he could to redeem Ruth, Boaz found a way forward by remembering how God described himself as compassionate *and* just in Exodus 34:

The LORD, the LORD, the compassionate and gracious
God, slow to anger, abounding in love and faithfulness,
maintaining love to thousands, and forgiving
wickedness, rebellion and sin. Yet he does not leave
the guilty unpunished; he punishes the children and
their children for the sin of the parents to the third and
fourth generation. (Exod. 34:6–7 NIV)

As we look out into our nation's future, full of elections, headlines, rallies, and marches, like Boaz, we can find a way forward, too. To light the path, we need voices that remind us God will justly judge our ability to obey his laws and voices that remind us that God will graciously pour out his compassion on our lives. Our conflict can act as a balancing rod, centering us on the tightrope anchored to honoring God's moral law on one end and showing God's love on the other. No earthly political party enjoys a biblical rightness monopoly. Neither a conservative nor a liberal belief system can fully embody God's endless grace and truth. When our friendships begin to suffer because our beliefs clash, the choice to love one another requires we remember that political debates will one day end. On that day, God will measure the depth of our obedience to him and the breadth of our care for others. Love and law matter eternally to God.

If loving people with differing political views seems like God expects us to achieve some spiritual body contortion act, I have good and bad news for us all. The bad news is that remaining in diverse friendships requires we bend in ways the world insists are impossible. But the (sort of) good news is that God has always expected his people to stretch and reach in this strange way. This stretch requires we embrace a peculiarity unlike any other faith system humans have historically upheld.

The Peculiarity of Our Faith

In his book *The Sacred Canopy*, author and sociologist Peter Berger, who critiqued both secular and religious thought, compares religion to a big umbrella or "canopy" that cultures set up over themselves to help themselves deal with death.[1] Berger explains the sociological understanding of religion involves four basic principles: (1) humans desire meaning in life; (2) we don't want that meaning in life to end; (3) we want our culture to last; (4) therefore, we construct a way to make it last by inventing an afterlife to help us deal with death. Sociologists then call these attempts to "deal with death" *religions*.

Berger says that because every religion is formed from one culture's attempt to deal with death and create meaning in life, each religion's followers are primarily members of its original, specific ethnic group or culture. The problem most religions face, then, is that if the original culture fades or dies, its religion dies with it. However, in contrast to these ethnically rooted religions, Berger highlights the uniqueness of "the historical peculiarity of Christianity."

Berger's use of this phrase points out that Christianity doesn't fit in the usual box sociologists use for religions because Christianity does not have a single, originating culture at its center. Although Jesus, the founder of Christianity, was Jewish, his fellow Jews rejected him as utterly non-Jewish based on his claim to be both God and human. And despite the beginning of Christianity in the Roman Empire, Rome crucified Jesus for treason and executed his followers regularly. In the earliest days of Christianity, Christians lived within political and cultural systems without submitting to them fully. They revered neither the Roman Caesar nor the Jewish high priest; they celebrated neither the Colosseum nor

---

[1]Peter L. Berger, *The Sacred Canopy: Elements of a Sociological Theory of Religion* (1967; reprint, New York: Anchor, 1991).

the temple. The culturally untethered new followers of Jesus survived and thrived, which seemed as unlikely as bacteria surviving in bleach.

Because of the "historical peculiarity" that neither Jesus nor his teachings were propped up by one culture, his following didn't arise from only one culture. After his resurrection, people from every ethnic background from all over the known world began to maintain a common faith. The world had never seen anything like it, as people from Europe to the Middle East to Africa began to follow Jesus.

A movement without a singular, definitive, and dominant culture became the most diverse faith system in the history of the world. Every other major world religion has maintained a geographically located cultural center—Buddhism and the Far East, Islam and the Middle East, Hinduism and India—but the Christian faith has not. Christianity began in the Middle East and then grew, stretched, and flourished into North Africa, Europe, Asia, and the Americas. How was this flourishing contortionist act achieved? In a way, it began with the early church following Boaz's lead and reaching any length necessary to cling to God's law and his love.

Keeping It Real

The early church spent much time grappling with how to love people from other cultures and backgrounds. Because its members maintained different cultural backgrounds and its churches existed in diverse cities, they faced many questions about which rules applied to whom and how they could love one another without letting go of God's law. For example, Paul wrote to the church in Rome regarding how they handled the Jewish law of circumcision when uncircumcised Gentiles came to faith in Christ. Judaism required circumcision, and many Jewish Christians thought Christianity should also require it. Circumcision did not make Jewish Christians uncomfortable, and requiring Gentile Christians in their churches to uphold circumcision asserted one cultural history as the dominant cultural norm. But Paul rightly understood that by creating a cultural center, they risked losing the power and peculiarity of salvation by faith through God's grace. Paul spoke of how their misguided practice of upholding laws apart from the grace of God created cultural polarization in this way:

> If you're brought up Jewish, don't assume that you can lean back in the arms of your religion and take it easy, feeling smug because you're an insider to God's revelation, a connoisseur of the best things of God, informed on the latest doctrines! I have a special word of caution for you who are sure that you have it all together yourselves and, because you know God's revealed Word inside and out, feel qualified to guide others through their blind alleys and dark nights and confused emotions to God. While you are guiding others, who is going to guide you? I'm quite serious. While preaching "Don't steal!" are you going to rob people blind? Who would suspect you? The same with adultery. The same with idolatry. You can get by with almost anything if you front it with eloquent talk about God and his law. The line from Scripture, "It's because of you Jews that the outsiders frown on God," shows it's an old problem that isn't going to go away. (Rom. 2:17–24 *The Message*)

Paul warned these early Christians not to make deals in the dark, to not pass off their cultural obedience as evidence of true salvation and devotion to God. Interestingly, this issue would not have arisen if their church hadn't been full of people of different ethnicities and backgrounds. Diversity didn't create a conflict between circumcised believers and uncircumcised believers. Instead, diversity exposed the natural human inclination to assume our experiences and beliefs should impact and possibly control the narrative of what it means to be human. If we believe we alone can determine how ideals like law and love ought to apply to everyone, we become blinded to where God's law and love intend to lead us: to a place of unrestrained trust and reliance on him.

To his great credit, Boaz's trust in God led everyone present at the town gates that day into the light with his commitment to hold together law and love. His actions approve what Paul later wrote in Romans 3:

> And where does that leave our proud Jewish claim of
> having a corner on God? Also canceled. God is the God
> of outsider non-Jews as well as insider Jews. How could
> it be otherwise since there is only one God? God sets
> right all who welcome his action and enter into it, both
> those who follow our religious system and those who
> have never heard of our religion.
>
> But by shifting our focus from what we do to what
> God does, don't we cancel out all our careful keeping of
> the rules and ways God commanded? Not at all. What
> happens, in fact, is that by putting that entire way of
> life in its proper place, we confirm it. (Rom. 3:29–31
> *The Message*)

Any time we feel tempted to view our churches as having insiders and outsiders of any category, whether that's political affiliation, race, ability, class, or anything else, we have Paul's letter to the Roman church and the life of Boaz to light the path toward honoring God's love and God's law. Paul and Boaz prioritized choosing to cling to relational connection to God and one another through their words, thoughts, and actions. Their faith in God's grace and his powerful truth held and healed whole communities when conflict and challenges came their way. We need that kind of faith in greater and greater measure as the twenty-first century progresses.

MORGAN

Juggling Conflict

The year 2020 was fraught with conflict for most churches, and Mosaic experienced the arguments and debates about how our church should respond to issues like the closing of schools and businesses, the wearing of masks, the ethics of vaccines, the validity of election results, and the state of policing in the United States. And depending on whom you talked to, we failed miserably at all of them. My pastoral inbox regularly filled with church members offering articles, videos, and other information they felt supported how our church ought to approach these hot topics.

Unfortunately, many of these articles, videos, or pieces of information disagreed about which approach and response best represented God's law and love. Pastoring a church in 2020 required a faith, wisdom, and resiliency no human could find without divine intervention.

One member of Mosaic regularly sent me all kinds of communication full of all kinds of advice. His confidence in his newly acquired expertise in all fields of study impressed me. His conviction that I must do exactly as he recommended bordered on manipulation and bullying. Several times, I had to graciously inform him that I disagreed with the experts from the videos he trusted implicitly. I stretched my love for him as I trusted God's ability to help us all find our way through that difficult time. We shared deep, complex discussions similar to the one at the beginning of this chapter. His perspective helped me understand some of the questions many other members were undoubtedly asking. Our leadership team carried his opinions and needs, along with many other people's, into every decision our elders made during that unprecedented time.

When Mosaic made a few key decisions this member didn't agree with, he left to find a church whose response to the trauma of 2020 lined up with his perspective. I don't know exactly what happened during his time away from Mosaic, but I do know that sometime in 2022, he returned and is flourishing in our community.

The lessons from Ruth helped me during those many months when, no matter what choice we made, someone in our church would be outraged or aghast while someone else would be equally relieved and overjoyed. Ruth is my favorite book of the Bible, perhaps because on dark days it offers me hope that whatever present trauma we face, making it through together will help us find a better ending. Ruth promises us that people return, and Ruth promises that God will use our kindness, generosity, and loyalty toward one another to accomplish a more just, righteous, and hopeful future.

But along with Ruth's narrative, I find encouragement that Christians can reach beyond their differences to walk forward together from times in church history when those who believed in Jesus clung to one another through times of cultural upheaval and change. One of those historic moments happened in 1974.

Putting It All Together

As he traveled around the world, Billy Graham noticed that many Christian leaders seemed disconnected from one another even as they approached furthering God's mission in the world. To bring God's people together, Graham organized a 1974 conference in

Lausanne, Switzerland, to connect global church leaders in humility, friendship, prayer, study, partnership, and hope. One critical question at the conference involved how the church of Jesus should move out into the world. What message and actions should they take to catalyze ministry worldwide? Should they focus on evangelism and gospel proclamation, as more traditionally conservative churches believed? Or should they focus on social work, feeding the poor, and speaking up for human rights, as more historically liberal churches believed? At its core, the conference sought to help Christians and churches worldwide hold God's law and love in equal honor.

The members of the congress struggled to find a path forward together until the leaders of churches from South and Central America stepped forward. With excellent theology and position papers steeped in the battlefields of poverty, human rights abuses, and the doctrinal errors taught by the colonizing churches on their continent, those brilliant and brave church leaders transformed the conference discussion to help create the Lausanne Covenant. Since its publication, this document has served as a North Star for Protestant churches.

We want to end this chapter with the paragraph from the Lausanne Covenant titled "Christian Social Responsibility." This paragraph was drafted initially by Latin American theologians and church leaders, edited by John Stott, affirmed by Billy Graham, and signed by evangelical leaders from more than 150 countries. We hope we will all find a way to remain faithful to this affirmation as we cling to Christ, who died because of his love for us and to fulfill the law, and to embrace one another, a peculiar people saved by grace through faith, to the very end.

We affirm that God is both the Creator and the Judge of all men. We therefore should share his concern for justice and reconciliation throughout human society and for the liberation of men from every kind of oppression. Because mankind is made in the image of God, every person, regardless of race, religion, colour, culture, class, sex or age, has an intrinsic dignity because of which he should be respected and served, not exploited. Here too we express penitence both for our neglect and for having sometimes regarded evangelism and social concern as mutually exclusive. Although reconciliation with man is not reconciliation with God, nor is social action evangelism, nor is political liberation salvation, nevertheless we affirm that evangelism and socio-political involvement are both part of our Christian duty. For both are necessary expressions of our doctrines of God and man, our love for our neighbour and our obedience to Jesus Christ. The message of salvation implies also a message of judgment upon every form of alienation, oppression and discrimination, and we should not be afraid to denounce evil and injustice wherever they exist. When people receive Christ they are born again into his kingdom and must seek not only to exhibit but also to spread its righteousness in the midst of an unrighteous world. The salvation we claim should be transforming us in the totality of our personal and social responsibilities. Faith without works is dead.[2]

---

[2]"The Lausanne Covenant," Lausanne Movement, https://lausanne.org/content/covenant/lausanne-covenant#cov.

STORIES
from our FRIENDS

A Heart for the Immigrant

BY CARLA

Mosaic was the first church I attended that portrayed racial reconciliation as part of the gospel and God's kingdom work. Of course, it makes sense that his plan involves all nations and all peoples coming together to form one global church body, but I had never seen that reality on display in one local church body.

I grew up in the 1980s in a border town where the United States and Mexico were separated only by the Rio Grande River, two cities and nations very much intertwined. I attended a Baptist school, but most of my friends and extended family were Catholic. My dad was a pastor at a small, Spanish-speaking, nondenominational church. Never once was race mentioned or addressed as part of God's plan for his kingdom, the gospel, or his church in any of those settings or relationships. Yet my city was rife with socioeconomic and racial divides.

After attending college in New York City, I moved to Austin, where I met my husband. He is a White Caucasian; I am a White Hispanic. I never thought we were an interracial couple until the first Mosaic community group we attended. One member remarked, "Hey, look, we're all interracial couples!" In that group, I listened intently as they openly shared the challenges of raising Black children and the hurdles racially and culturally blended families face. Many of these friends were weary of brothers and sisters in Christ adamantly denying that racism exists and of the struggle required to stay in a diverse church, where they couldn't retreat to the comfort of a monoracial shared identity.

These conversations with my Black friends revealed my blind spots about racism. When they extended forgiveness and grace for my ignorance about their experiences, I learned to do the same for those who don't understand the plight of the immigrant. I often struggle when Christians make disparaging remarks about undocumented persons. I was born in the United States, grew up on the Mexican side of the US–Mexico border, and crossed it every day to go to school in the United States. The border to me was fluid; both cities created one larger community with separate governments and infrastructures but with the same families who had known each other for years. Even to this day, it is hard to say definitively where I am from because I feel both cities are home.

Growing up, when I observed people living without electricity or running water in cardboard or makeshift houses and dirt streets, I understood only God's grace allowed me to be born into a family with means and born in the United States with every opportunity that citizenship afforded me. As a result, I take offense when people look down upon Latin American immigrants or other undocumented persons fleeing poverty, war, and violence. I feel anger when I hear Christians say that they "worked hard," did things "the right way," and all these "illegals" should be punished and deported. What if they had been born somewhere else? Immigration is not simply a political issue for me—it is spiritual and emotional.

Being a part of a multiethnic community is not unlike life in two border towns. Witnessing and sharing our different backgrounds and experiences creates a relational fluidity that enhances our ability to experience the gospel in new ways. My diverse friendships made and make me better. They expose areas where I need God's forgiveness, grace, and maturity to help me extend love, compassion, and forgiveness toward others.

Chapter 10

BETHLEHEM'S CHOICE

Looking to the Past

Then the elders and all the people at the gate said, "We are witnesses. May the LORD make the woman who is coming into your home like Rachel and Leah . . . may your family be like that of Perez, whom Tamar bore to Judah."

—Ruth 4:11–12 NIV

Hopefully, we have shown that the book of Ruth isn't merely a story about individual lives but is actually a story about how the choices and stories of individual people create a collective framework to support God's grander tale of redemption and rescue. Here in Ruth 4, as the narrative hurtles toward its incredible climax, it is time for our main characters to step back for a moment, and it is time for the townspeople of Bethlehem to step up, take center stage, and play their part. Just as Ruth's appeal to Boaz forced Boaz to make a complicated decision, Boaz's response to Ruth asked the little town of Bethlehem to make one as well. At the town gate, Boaz asked the city leaders to weigh in on the possibility of his being the *go-el* for Elimelech's family by marrying

Ruth. This proposal created a tricky spot and sticky space for the people of Bethlehem. Approving his marriage to a Jewish widow would be one thing. But bringing a racial, cultural, and religious outsider from their enemy nation of Moab into the center of their people asked a lot of them.

When pressed to make this decision, what would they do? When asked to consider making space for a multiethnic future in their midst, what could they look to for guidance? Who could they turn to when asked to approve an interracial marriage between a powerful landowner and a poor refugee? The people of Bethlehem looked to the past and gave their ancestors a seat at the decision-making table:

> All the people who were in the court, and the elders,
> said, "We are witnesses. May the LORD make the woman
> who is coming into your home like Rachel and Leah,
> both of whom built the house of Israel." (Ruth 4:11 NASB)

In a crucial moment, they affirmed the need for a kind of multi-generational wisdom to help inform their decision in the present, and they said yes to Ruth. By doing so, the Bethlehemites accomplished the following:

- They didn't shun the refugee coming to them.
- They didn't close the halls of power to the poor.
- They didn't withhold provision from the widow.
- They didn't give in to xenophobia (fear of foreigners).
- They didn't force Ruth back into the shadows, condemned to a life of gleaning scraps.

How did the people of Bethlehem overcome all the possible selfish, sinful endings to Ruth's story and wind up creating space for a new and better end for everyone involved?

In making their decision, the people of Bethlehem looked to three women in their history and allowed the lessons from those women's lives to shape their own.

Women as Nation Builders

For the Jewish audience first exposed to the book of Ruth, the implications of the callback to Leah and Rachel would have been obvious. We can read in depth the story of Leah and Rachel in Genesis. But for our purposes, the essential fact is that they were sisters who married the same man, Jacob.

Certainly, we should briefly address polygamy before moving forward regarding Leah and Rachel. While polygamy was a commonly expressed cultural institution in the ancient Near East, God (Yahweh) never affirmed the institution and moved people away from polygamy many times. The Old Testament accounts of polygamy in the Hebrew scriptures often act as an ancient equivalent of a 1980s "don't do drugs" after-school special, exposing the pain polygamy brought upon families. "Don't Do Polygamy" could be the title of any number of Bible stories, including the one about Leah and Rachel attempting to prove their worth to their husband through the production of heirs.

Putting aside the relational anguish of Leah and Rachel's story, the townspeople of Bethlehem specifically pointed to Leah and Rachel's roles as nation builders when they said these women "built the house of Israel." Abraham's twelve great-grandsons born through Leah and Rachel effectively laid the groundwork for an explosion of Hebrew people on the earth. These sisters were national heroes.

Hundreds of years later, when the townspeople of Bethlehem considered bringing Ruth into their community, they looked back at Leah and Rachel and spoke a blessing over Ruth: *May Ruth become a hero who shapes and impacts our nation.* In a culture that deeply valued generational flourishing and producing heirs, Bethlehem affirmed Ruth as a potential future matriarch.

MORGAN

Shuffling Generations

This story of cross-generational love and support reminds me of a challenge I faced when I first became the pastor of Mosaic in my early thirties. I realized quickly I had little power to change one weakness as a leader: my young age. I learned well that when a thirty-four-year-old first-time pastor replaces a sixty-something experienced pastor, the generation gap experienced by the congregation feels as wide as the sides of the Grand Canyon, or maybe even the Milky Way.

The gap between the previous pastor and me was vast. Sermon illustrations from television: *Black-ish* versus *The Flintstones*. Approach to life: naïveté versus wisdom. What the congregation saw: a whippersnapper versus a sage. It got choppy, and I wearied of being asked by visitors if I was the youth pastor (no offense whatsoever to all the incredible youth/student pastors out there; you make the world go around and endure the slings and arrows of outrageous parents).

As more gray heads were leaving than I could count, I tried to keep up with them through countless breakfast and lunch meetings. However, my bad sermons and limited leadership experience had taken its toll, and they moved on to churches with less-green pastors.

Then a third-quarter-in-life saint named Don arrived in my life. Don was a big-time professional in his field, and he had a soft spot for the young guy. When we talked, he continually encouraged me with words like: *Don't worry about everyone else, you're doing a great job! I believe in you!*

Despite the disconnect between our generational experiences and perspectives, Don courageously hit the shuffle button on his life's church leadership playlist. He wasn't used to listening to Gen X culture references. He didn't personally connect with my stage of life, which involved toddler tantrums and navigating a huge learning curve professionally. Nor was Don familiar with the vision God had placed in my heart to see God's love for a diverse people displayed in our congregation. But Don miraculously chose to shuffle my stories, dreams, and ideas in with his own. And the lesson he taught me about humility and honor was greatly needed.

Don's consistent encouragement and faithfulness emboldened me to get up one Sunday and address the generational elephant in the room: "I know that most of you aren't used to your pastor being younger than you are. But unless you live to be ninety-five, and your pastor is ninety-six, at some point, if you stay on this side of glory, your pastor will be younger than you. It's just a fact. So, congratulations! Today is that day!"

I'm not sure every boomer in the room laughed as much as I did at that, but Don's friendship filled me with the courage to be secure about who I was and what God had called me to do. His friendship emboldened me to ask for grace from the people of a different generation. I genuinely believe that if Don hadn't hit the "shuffle button" with me, and if I hadn't reciprocated, our church would not have grown into what it has become. A willingness to shuffle the perspectives and experiences of older and younger generations into our own is essential in a multigenerational church.

Say It Five Times Fast

Interestingly, Wesleyan theology offers us a tool that facilitates connecting across generational lines, and it's older than every single person in every church in the world. This tool is called the

Wesleyan Quadrilateral (say it five times fast), and it functions as a decision-making grid developed to help the people of God push the shuffle button as they navigate tricky times and sticky theological and moral spots. Four elements make up the four "sides" of this grid: reason, experience, Scripture, and tradition. When we come to any complicated question, this four-sided tool reminds us to apply our minds (reason), our personal history (experience), the Word of God (Scripture), and what has been said or done in the past that speaks to the question at hand (tradition). This produces a holistic approach to Bible interpretation and decision-making that does not discount the self, other people impacted by the decision, or God.

Perhaps the most surprising and challenging side of the Wesleyan Quadrilateral is that of "tradition," which asks us to look to the past to help us understand the present. As modern people, we tend to leave the past in the past and assume we are wiser and better than anyone who came before us, simply because we lived after them and have things like indoor plumbing and Google. (Let's not ask Augustine or Einstein how they might feel about this; I don't think our pride could handle their scorn.) C. S. Lewis (another brilliant mind, despite living long before smartphones existed) coined a term for this bias: chronological snobbery. Since no one wants to commit snobbery, the Wesleyan Quadrilateral comes to our rescue and insists we give our ancestors a seat at the table.

Bethlehem's instinct to hold up its tradition regarding Ruth aligns with the wisdom of the Wesleyan Quadrilateral. There was one minor hiccup, however, in the seat Bethlehem offered Ruth at its table. But before we grapple with that, we'd like to tell you about some tables we set at Mosaic and what God built through the people sitting at them.

The Gospel and . . .

On August 9, 2014, Michael Brown, an unarmed, Black, eighteen-year-old teenager, was shot and killed by police in Ferguson, Missouri, after Brown reportedly robbed a convenience store. In the days that followed, protests and civil unrest dominated Ferguson and ignited another national conversation and debate about race relations and the police's use of force against African Americans in the United States.

The debate raged online and on social media platforms, and none of the discourse seemed to have positive results. Friends turned on friends, insults abounded, hurts were exposed and expressed, and people seemed to be retreating to well-established ethnic silos.

Discouragingly, much of this was happening in our church, even among people with a long history of multiethnic relationships. Friendships that had flourished for years were fraying and at their breaking point as people on both sides of the debate considered walking away from a long-held dream of a multiethnic faith community.

What could change the situation? What could turn it around and begin to give hope and perhaps heal hearts?

After several months of conversation, Mosaic launched a series of meetings called "The Gospel and . . ." (also known as TGA). The idea behind TGA was simple but risky:

- Choose a challenging topic involving race, ethnicity, or diversity.
- Gather people at the church on a Friday night.
- Teach briefly on the topic.
- Allow people to discuss their experiences and perspectives in depth in smaller groups.

If you think this idea sounds like a solid opportunity for people to misunderstand, frustrate, and need to forgive one another, you aren't wrong. We processed many missteps, miscalculations, misunderstandings, and mistakes made along the way. A few people left Mosaic over TGA, claiming we had "abandoned the gospel in favor of diversity." But far more people followed the path of Bethlehem, looked to the past, and opened their arms to bless one another. Consider this story from one White male TGA participant:

> Selfishly, I keep coming back [to TGA] so that I don't have to live in ignorance anymore. I did not grow up in a diverse environment. I still remember a story that [a Black female leader] told. She told a story and asked all the people at her table how they would respond—and all of the White people responded one way, and all the Black people responded another.
>
> She said that her son, a twenty-one-year-old African American male, was at a party, and when people began drinking heavily, he turned to leave. At that point, a friend of his came up and asked if he would drive home two heavily drunk White women. Then she asked the table, if he were your son, what would you encourage him to do?
>
> All the White people instantly said, "He should have driven them home." But all the Black people instantly and emotionally reacted negatively, and said, "No way should he ever drive them home!" I didn't understand, but they asked me, "What if he had been pulled over on the way home with two drunk White girls in his car? What do you think that looks like and what do you think the police could have done to him?"

I didn't even think about how ethnicity affects that kind of choice.

No wonder someone like Michael Emerson, a leading researcher on race and religion, writes:

> Involvement in multiracial congregations, over time, leads to fundamental differences. Friendship patterns change. Through national surveys we find that people in multiracial congregations have significantly more friendships across race than do other Americans. For example, for those attending racially homogenous congregations, 83 percent said most or all of their friends were the same race as them. For those not attending any congregation, 70 percent said most or all of their friends were the same race as them.
>
> But for those attending multiracial congregations, there is a dramatic difference. Only 36 percent of people attending racially mixed congregations said most or all of their friends were the same race as them. And we found that those 36 percent were relatively recent arrivals to their racially mixed congregations.[1]

Our conversations about loving one another at TGA created a "Bethlehem town gate" environment in our community. We pointed to cultural conflicts and misunderstandings surrounding diversity and invited Jesus to the table to help us find a gospel-centered response. Sunday mornings remained as the day our spiritual family gathered to worship God together. But those quarterly Friday nights became opportunities to share a table to talk about

---

[1] Michael O. Emerson, "A New Day for Multiracial Congregations," *Reflections* (Spring 2013), http://reflections.yale.edu/article/future-race/new-day-multiracial-congregations.

how our past experiences affected our present perspectives so we could try to find our way into the future together (which we will discuss more in Chapter Eleven).

When the people of Bethlehem held up Leah and Rachel at their discussion to bless Ruth, though, they couldn't ignore one stark contrast between Ruth and those women: Ruth wasn't Jewish. How, then, could she be the mother of Israel's future? How could she qualify to one day sit at the table with Leah and Rachel? Before the townspeople of Bethlehem could begin their future together with their newly anointed Leah-and-Rachel-like friend Ruth, they had to look to the past again to find precedence for embracing an ethnic outsider as one of their own.

Tamar and Breakthrough

If the people of Bethlehem allowed Rachel and Leah a seat at the table as they affirmed Boaz and Ruth's union, they practically rented a room out to someone else. Let's be honest and acknowledge, as readers, we probably didn't see her name coming. And yet, the people of Bethlehem said, "Moreover, may your house be like the house of Perez whom Tamar bore to Judah, through the offspring which the Lord will give you by this young woman" (Ruth 4:12 NASB1995).

Tamar's life offers another sticky, tricky, saucy story of grace. She lived a generation beyond Leah and Rachel's lives. Leah's son Judah (by all accounts, a horrible man for much of his life) had a son named Er. Judah arranged for Er to marry Tamar, who was a Canaanite. Genesis 38:7 declares Er was so wicked that God abruptly ended his life. Er and Tamar had not produced children, so Judah commanded his second son, Onan, to have sex with Tamar to continue his brother's line.

If Judah's plan sounds familiar, it's because Judah used the same cultural move that compelled Boaz to redeem Naomi's line and take Ruth as his wife. In Judah's day, this practice existed as an expected custom; by Boaz's day, it had been codified as Jewish law. However, unlike Boaz, Onan wouldn't do it.

> But Onan knew that the child would not be his; so whenever he slept with his brother's wife, he spilled his semen on the ground to keep from providing offspring for his brother. What he did was wicked in the LORD's sight; so the LORD put him to death also. (Gen. 38:9–10 NIV)

The men with the power and privilege necessary to protect and care for Tamar had failed her twice, and God had ended both men's lives. Now doubly widowed, Tamar became undesirable to her father-in-law, Judah. Judah scorned the responsibility to provide care and provision for Tamar and sent her home to live with her family until his third son could marry her.

Many years passed, and Judah's own wife died. Legally, at this point, Judah could have married Tamar himself to continue Er's lineage. But Judah did not do this, nor did he send for her when his third son, Shelah, grew up.

Eventually, Tamar heard Judah planned to be at a big sheep-shearing party in Timnah (Gen. 38:12). Tamar, who remained Judah's responsibility, took matters into her own hands. She veiled herself as a prostitute and sat by the road to Timnah, where Judah offered her a goat in exchange for sex. However, since Judah did not have the goat with him, Tamar asked for his staff and seal (an ancient form of proof of identification) as a pledge and proof that he owed her something. Judah later sent the goat as payment, but the mystery woman from the side of the road could not be found. Judah realized that if people learned he had, in effect, lost his wallet and credit card to an unnamed woman, he would have "become a laughingstock" (Gen. 38:23 NIV).

At this point, let's consider the cunning character of Tamar. She knew her father-in-law well, rightly predicting he would solicit a prostitute when given a chance. She correctly assumed his regard for her was so low and his notice of her so vaporous that he would not recognize her voice or body. Tamar predicted he would not offer her any form of payment he had with him then, and therefore she would be able to procure proof of their sexual encounter. Tamar had no power to ensure her survival and no prospects for her future provision, but Tamar knew the law and what she was due as a member of Judah's family. Although she used deception to obtain what was rightfully hers, it seems unlikely anything else would have persuaded Judah to honor what was right and godly otherwise.

Three months later, Judah heard Tamar was pregnant after prostituting herself. With his "honor" threatened by his daughter-in-law's sin, Judah called her out of hiding to burn her to death. Judah, the man who had once used his authority and privilege to sell his brother Joseph into slavery, now ordered someone to set fire to a pregnant woman.

The contrast between Judah and Boaz is shocking. Judah disrespected women and refused to provide for his closest family members as the law required. Boaz protected and honored women, and then he provided for distant relatives because the law said he should. Judah sought out a prostitute for sex because he could, and he then condemned a pregnant (alleged) prostitute to death. Boaz refused to have sex with a woman he loved, and he then bought her family land and allowed their sons to carry on Elimelech's name.

The similarities between Ruth and Tamar are equally striking. Both women were foreigners married to descendants of Abraham. Both women were widows and entirely dependent on others for their survival. Both offered themselves to powerful men from their husbands' families. Their stories diverge due to the differing character of the men with the power and privilege necessary to help them. Ruth's story ends with a happily ever after; Tamar's ending is bittersweet, to say the least.

Judah did eventually face his sin and cruelty. Before she could be executed, Tamar produced his seal and staff as proof of his paternity. Judah knew he'd been caught red-handed and declared the punch line to the whole story: "She is more righteous [*tsadaq*] than I" (Gen. 38:26 NIV). Let's not miss this ancient Jewish man's boldness when he declared a Canaanite woman's righteousness greater than his own. Nor should we overlook the parallel between Judah's praise of Tamar and Boaz's praise of Ruth in Ruth 3:11. Judah never slept with Tamar again after he realized he had fathered her child. This fact implies that his respect and honor for Tamar freed her from functioning as sexual property to be passed around in his family. As we said, this was a bittersweet ending for a woman who endured significant trauma in her life.

Commentators point to the twin boys Tamar birthed, Perez and Zerah, as a kind of redemption for Judah's dead sons, who had failed to love and honor Tamar. Perez means "breakthrough" and Zerah means "brightness." Considering these names in light of the horrific pain she endured in Judah's family, it's easy to hope her sons' love for her consoled and comforted her. We don't know what their relationships were like, but we do know Tamar's family continued, and Judah's house was unforgettably restored by her life and choices, as complicated as they were.

Perhaps the people of Bethlehem made space for Ruth's complicated circumstances because Tamar's story taught them that love and justice involve complex, painful stories of breakthroughs that light the darkness. And maybe, that lesson highlighted for them how love and justice are often more complex and painful than we'd like them to be.

What Justice Can't Do

Judah and Tamar's sordid tale is a remarkable story about how far God commands we ought to go as we pursue justice. As Americans, our culture's generalized view of justice is that it exists to either (1) guarantee individual rights or (2) attempt to make up for something lost, as when a guilty person is punished for a misdeed.

However, the Bible's view of justice (*mishpat*) is far more expansive. Biblical justice concerns itself as much with what we all owe one another as humans made in the image of God as it does with what the guilty owe their victims or society to make up for their wrongdoing. Throughout the Bible, God critiqued the injustice of his people when they withheld something from the vulnerable: money, rights, care, space, provision, etc.

God does this so often that one theologian used another four-sided grid to define those deserving of our help and resources. In his book, *Justice: Rights and Wrongs*, Nicholas Wolterstorff calls his grid the "quartet of the vulnerable."[2] He points to how God lifts up four people groups over and over as deserving of justice: the poor, widows, orphans, and immigrants. Bible justice looks as much or more like releasing our resources into the lives of those in vulnerable positions than it does in merely punishing wrongdoers, despite how crucial societal order is in any city or nation.

Punishment for the guilty is necessary and right, but the painful, complex truth about justice is that punishment for past actions can never make up for lost life or opportunity. For example, when a child is killed, no amount of jail time served by the murderer or money paid in a civil settlement can bring back a family's precious son or daughter. In every circumstance involving another person's victimization, it would always be better if the

---

[2] Nicholas Wolterstorff, *Justice: Rights and Wrongs* (Princeton, NJ: Princeton University Press, 2008).

wrongdoing or injustice were never committed in the first place. Lament begins when we recognize the impossibility of bringing back what was lost.

At the center of any painful injustice lies a deep well of grief. When we take time to discuss injustices, we hear echoes of sorrow carried by the people whose ancestors suffered through those traumatic histories. This is why our understanding of past injustices such as the oppression of Indigenous Americans, the Atlantic slave trade, two hundred years of slavery in the United States, the internment of Japanese Americans during World War II, the Holocaust, Jim Crow laws, the effects of patriarchal ideas and practices, and others is important. Just as no form of justice can replace a lost child, humankind cannot undo all the wrongs we have allowed or perpetuated. But like the people of Bethlehem, who honored Rachel, Leah, and Tamar for building their nation despite their unjust, painful circumstances, we can honor the people who endured injustice as heroes by validating their loss and suffering as we strive to build a more just society. When we pursue justice for others like them, we show we understand they birthed this future through the pain they endured.

Looking at and talking about the past to help us understand what to do in the present isn't left-wing or right-wing; it isn't woke or anti-woke; it's simply wise and biblical. Remembering the failures of the past helps us do better now, in the present. The people of Bethlehem could have been like Judah, who said no to caring for and embracing Tamar as one who belonged. Judah took a long time to do what was right and honor Tamar as more righteous than himself. All that time cost him two sons and his reputation. That same time brought years of suffering and humiliation into Tamar's life. Who can read the story without longing for Judah to make a better choice from the beginning? While no amount of justice could change Judah's choice, the Bethlehemites looked back at the pain created by Tamar's rejection in the past and chose to see Ruth as a person worthy of honor and care in the present. When they said yes to Ruth with open arms, they played a part in the glory yet to come.

The Star of Bethlehem

Let's not forget that the book of Ruth is, once more, set against the backdrop of the time of the judges. Terrible tales of sex, violence, and revenge fill the book of Judges. The graphic savagery of its stories reminds us how low and far the people of Israel had fallen. Judges ended with the Israelites gone wrong; the story of Ruth sits in the middle of that broken time and presents a tale of townspeople doing right. Contrasted with the depravity in Judges, Bethlehem's warm embrace of Ruth is a shining star of courage and justice. Their actions prove that faithful people remain loyal to God's ways, even in the darkest of times.

God ultimately honored Bethlehem for pursuing justice, hitting shuffle to let their past generations shape their present choices, and embracing a vulnerable woman as a future hero. God chose Bethlehem to be the birthplace of the legendary King David a few generations later. Much later, God's favor overflowed in abundance toward this town that heralded Leah, Rachel, and Tamar as heroes and celebrated a widowed Moabite. When God chose his Son's birthplace, he led Mary and Joseph to Bethlehem. This town, known as the "House of Bread," where two impoverished widows once gleaned grain to survive, became the town where the Bread of Life was born. Spiritually, anyone who calls on the name of Jesus gleans from Bethlehem's gracious generosity toward outsiders.

Some might call God's favor toward Bethlehem a bold message about how far God will go to honor a people's pursuit of doing the right thing. When we consider Jesus's teaching from Matthew 25, the birth of Jesus in Bethlehem seems like an obvious choice for God. Jesus said that when we feed the hungry, give water to the thirsty, clothe the naked, house foreigners, and tend to the sick and prisoners, he personally receives all our care. When God favored Bethlehem in Jesus's day, perhaps it was because it was a place God had experienced deep and meaningful care when the little town loved a poor immigrant in Ruth and Naomi's day.

May we love God well by loving the needy. May we honor the past by lamenting its grief. And may God's favor toward our lives and churches lead us into a redemptive, multigenerational future beyond any breakthrough we could have imagined on this side of glory.

STORIES
from our FRIENDS

A Marvelous Generational Blessing

BY JACK HAMMANS

When my wife, Oneta, and I began attending Mosaic Church of Austin in 2018, it was apparent there were not many gray-haired, slightly stooped senior citizens like us in the congregation. This fact did not in the slightest deter us from becoming members of the church. We soon joined a thriving community group that was truly multigenerational; approximately a third of those attending were over fifty. We felt entirely accepted, and our participation in group discussions and prayer times was well-received.

I had recently retired from a long career in pastoral ministry, but I had no intention of resting on my laurels. I was more than willing to serve our new community of Jesus followers—as long as it did not involve attending board meetings or doing marriage counseling! I was grateful for the opportunities to minister through teaching and mentoring a few young men in the church. Granted, one was fifty years old, but he seemed young to me!

In the late spring of 2020, one of Mosaic's associate pastors asked if I would serve as a guest teacher at a young adults community group. The group, led by a young man named Christian, was studying Romans and had reached chapter 9, a vexing "problem passage" of the letter. For centuries, Romans 9 has been a theological battleground, and Christian had asked the pastor to speak to the group, but since that pastor had a prior commitment, he told Christian, "I know just the guy you need" and recommended me.

I accepted the invitation, but not without some nervousness. I was a complete unknown to the group, and I was coming as a "ringer." They were all twentysomethings; I was a septuagenarian, half a century older than they. Because of the COVID-19 epidemic, the session would be held remotely via Zoom, which could hinder the early establishment of rapport. An email exchange with Christian gave me some helpful background on the group. However, I was still a bit concerned about how well this group of youngsters and this old guy, a total stranger, could relate to each other.

The evening could not have gone better! The ice was quickly broken by Christian's warm and respectful greeting and my slightly humorous self-introduction. After a few minutes of "catching up" with the group members, I was given the floor. I attempted to offer a "fair and balanced" look at various interpretations of Romans 9–11. Some group members asked thoughtful and incisive questions. The last part of the meeting was devoted to sharing prayer requests and intercession for one another. The prayer requests were personal and non-superficial. I was also asked if I needed prayer about anything. It seemed to me that this band of twentysomethings was committed to "a long obedience in the same direction." Whatever spiritual benefit I provided to the group was well reciprocated. They ministered to me as much as I ministered to them. This bridging of the "generation gap" by mutual acceptance, honor, and service in authentic body life at Mosaic is the Lord's doing and is marvelous in our eyes!

OUR CHOICE

Loving into the Future

The women said to Naomi: "Praise be to the LORD, who this day has not left you without a guardian-redeemer. May he become famous throughout Israel! He will renew your life and sustain you in your old age."

—Ruth 4:14–15 NIV

In arguably the most moving image in the book of Ruth, the final scene paints a happily ever after future. Like a couple from a Hollywood fairy tale, the reader finds that Boaz and Ruth have married and produced a son. The happy couple stands beside Naomi, who was once bitter and empty but now has a lap full of legacy. We watch as Naomi bounces Ruth's baby on her knees, with her old friends gathered around her in the ultimate happy ending.

Naomi's chorus of friends then blessed her guardian-redeemer in Ruth 4:14: "Praise be to the LORD, who this day has not left you without a guardian-redeemer. May he become famous throughout Israel" (NIV). At first glance, these women seem to be singing Boaz's praises, declaring him the greatest guardian-redeemer of all time. To remix the old hymn, the women seem to be singing, *What a friend we have in Boaz, all our pains and poverty to bear; what a privilege to know him, he is the answer to our prayers.*

But if we assume Naomi's friends were singing Boaz's praises, we'd be wrong. Naomi's backup singers went on to say, "He will renew your life and sustain you in your old age. For your daughter-in-law, who loves you and who is better to you than seven sons, has given him birth" (Ruth 4:15 NIV).

Wait. Full stop.

Ruth didn't give birth to Boaz, so clearly, the women weren't hyping him up as Naomi's ultimate guardian-redeemer. Who were these women singing about? Who is the one they claimed would fully redeem Naomi's life?

Her friends didn't sing about Boaz; they sang about the baby.

How is Ruth's baby the unexpected, ultimate redeemer in the book of Ruth?

A Neon Sign

You might have seen the data: the United States will become increasingly diverse in the coming decades. According to Pew Research, future immigrants and their descendants are expected to account for 88 percent of the United States' population growth through 2065.[1] We are undoubtedly headed toward an increasingly racially diverse future, and the friendships we prioritize today will prepare us for a tomorrow we can only try to imagine.

In a way, the stunning twist of Naomi's grandson as the future redeemer provides proof of God's redemption and challenges us to see the vital role of our diverse friendships in what is to come. After Naomi's friends sing about a redeemer and the book of Ruth

---

[1]Abby Budiman, "Key Findings about U.S. Immigrants," Pew Research Center, August 20, 2020, https://www.pewresearch.org/fact-tank/2020/08/20/key-findings-about-u-s-immigrants/.

rolls its final credits, we encounter a kind of postlude, or a "what happened to our main characters" moment. If we scroll down the final page in Ruth 4, we find a genealogy meant to ensure we get the point of the whole story: "So they named him [Boaz and Ruth's son] Obed. He is the father of Jesse, the father of David" (Ruth 4:17 NASB).

In those words, the author of Ruth shines a light to show us the way to the future. Like that Christmas star hanging over Bethlehem, a neon sign was hanging over baby Obed's head, pointing to a future redeemer: King David. *This story isn't just about us,* these women insisted. *Your redemption isn't just about you; it's also about all the generations ahead.*

King David, like Boaz, qualified as a mini-redeemer. David ruled for a finite amount of time, accomplished some amazing things, and also failed miserably on occasion. David lived the life of a onetime king who united peoples during his lifetime. He became famous in his day for his exploits, but his everlasting fame hinged on his connection to someone else.

David would have remained a relatively obscure king from a global viewpoint if it weren't for the birth of another baby in Bethlehem many generations later. From an Old Testament perspective, Ruth's genealogy holds David up as a bridge to a future Naomi's friends could sense but could never imagine. But Naomi's friends didn't know about the someday King David. The author added it later to help us connect the dots those women could not see.

What bridge connected their hearts to the future redemption God had planned? To find it, let us introduce you to the life of one German Jew and the unexpected bridge that carried his heart to healing.

The Magic of Friendship

In a 2019 TED Talk with well over one million views, a man named Eddie Jaku told the horrifying and true story of his imprisonment in Nazi work camps during World War II.[2] Once his physical suffering ended, Jaku suffered mentally, as he carried the weight of hatred and horror from his trauma. Like Naomi, Jaku credited holding his firstborn son with the moment he began to believe he could be happy again. Eddie Jaku found hope for future redemption by holding a baby in his arms. In both ancient Bethlehem and modern Europe, a baby offered a bridge over troubled waters, out of loss and suffering. And how did Eddie Jaku claim he made it all the way to that bridge? Like Ruth and Naomi, one gift in life became Jaku's source of strength and courage necessary to survive. What was that gift?

You guessed it: friendship.

In his memoir, *The Happiest Man on Earth*, Jaku tells the story of his friendship with a fellow prisoner, Kurt Hirschfeld.[3] Jaku was often tempted to end his life to escape the horrors of Auschwitz but credited his survival to the simple knowledge that his friend Kurt cared for him and required care in return. In his TED Talk, Eddie Jaku said this about friendship:

> One flower is my garden; one good friend is my world. . . . I wonder how people exist without friendship, without people to share their secrets, hopes, and dreams, to share good fortune or sad losses. In the sweetness of friendship, let there be laughter and sharing of pleasure, good times

---

[2] Eddie Jaku, "The Happiest Man on Earth: 99 Year Old Holocaust Survivor Shares His Story," TEDxSydney, July 18, 2019, https://www.youtube.com/watch?v=scCvi3vY4jQ.

[3] Eddie Jaku, *The Happiest Man on Earth: The Beautiful Life of an Auschwitz Survivor* (London: Macmillan, 2020).

made better and bad times forgotten—due to the magic of friendship.[4]

Without the smaller world created by Hirschfeld's unbreakable friendship, Jaku would not have survived to be liberated, meet his wife, and father his children, grandchildren, and great-grandchildren. One friendship became the bridge between Eddie Jaku's hell on Earth and a future full of hope and love.

Jaku calls the empowering connection shared by two friends a kind of magic, but the Bible would use a different word to describe the powerful, transformative, life-giving, and restorative quality of our friendships. In Ephesians, we learn that the work friendship can do in the world is more mystery than magic.

MORGAN

Paul and the Mystery of Friendship

I do love a good mystery. I grew up reading all the mysteries I could get my hands on from the library, and I still love detective characters, shows, and books. Carrie and I enjoy watching mystery TV shows and movies; however, she's much more successful at guessing whodunit. My competitive nature refuses to attempt to deduce the answer to the mystery (mostly because I never get it right, and the "losing" is too painful). As a result, I don't see a mystery as a chance to guess the author's story before the author tells it. A good mystery allows me to enjoy unexpected twists and turns until the revelatory ending when the villain is unmasked, and the author and I celebrate together. Hooray, everyone!

But modern mysteries and New Testament mysteries aren't the same. Primarily, New Testament mysteries are concepts that once were concealed but now are revealed right in the middle of

---

[4] Jaku, "The Happiest Man on Earth," 8:45, 9:30.

history—not at the end of the world's story. For example, consider three main "revealed mysteries" the Christian faith has introduced to the world: the Trinitarian nature of God by which we understand God's three-in-oneness (Matt. 28:19), the hypostatic union of Christ by which we understand Jesus was and is fully God and fully human (1 Tim. 3:16), and what Paul introduced us to in Ephesians 3: the mystery of the diverse, multiethnic church.

Nosebleed-section theology on what and who the church is opened the letter in Ephesians 1 and 2. But before Paul could get to more practical matters in chapters 4–6, he got a little choked up writing about something specific and took a detour with a single phrase in Ephesians 3:1: "For this reason I, Paul, the prisoner of Christ Jesus for the sake of you Gentiles—" (NIV). And just like that, with a single dash after the word "Gentiles," we find ourselves invited on a journey into the heart of a Bible mystery:

> Surely you have heard about the administration of God's grace that was given to me for you, that is, the mystery made known to me by revelation, as I have already written briefly. (Eph. 3:2–3 NIV)

The mystery Paul spoke of is that now—not before—but only now in Jesus Christ, the multiethnic church can exist. And this mystery is so central to the gospel message that Paul calls this mystery the very "mystery of Christ":

> In reading this, then, you will be able to understand my insight into the mystery of Christ, which was not made known to people in other generations as it has now been revealed by the Spirit to God's holy apostles and prophets. (Eph. 3:4–5 NIV)

Paul not only named and defined the mystery, but he also gave us the answer to the whodunit: "This mystery is that through the gospel the Gentiles are heirs together with Israel, members together of one body, and sharers together in the promise in Christ Jesus" (Eph. 3:6 NIV). Paul insisted that the story of the church didn't end when the mystery was revealed; instead, the story of the church began with the revelation of a new mystery altogether. Instead of ending the mystery by exposing who was to blame, the church began when it was revealed who would be in God's family.

Paul saw that God had always planned to create a diverse, multiethnic body of people. This "insight" so deeply impacted Paul that he left behind his former life, laid down his pride in his cultural and racial identity, and allowed himself to even be imprisoned for the sake of the Gentiles. For the sake of new friends, those he had not yet made, and those he might never meet, Paul went to prison and went to work saving lives.

The Tension in the Mystery

It should be acknowledged that an inherent tension sits at the center of all great gospel mysteries. Should we try to resolve the tension created by the complexity of our Trinitarian belief by flattening God into one person alone (unipersonalism) or smashing him into one person with three different faces (modalism), our understanding of God collapses into heresy. Likewise, if we try to resolve the inherent tension at the heart of the hypostatic union of Christ by emphasizing his divinity more than his humanity or vice versa, our understanding of Christ collapses into heresy.

Similarly, if we try to resolve the tension brought about by the inherent ethnic, racial, and cultural diversity in the church of Jesus, our understanding of the multiethnic church will collapse. Throughout the ages, many Christians have, understandably, tried to resolve this tension—most often by trying to escape it. To understand why so few churches are diverse in the United States, we need look no further than the governing principle put at the center of many US churches called the Homogeneous Unit Principle (HUP).

Developed by US church growth experts in the middle to late twentieth century, the HUP makes the case that churches will grow fastest and reach the most people by encouraging their people to reach others just like themselves. And while that kind of gospel aim can be good in countless ways (and resolves the uncomfortable tensions that lie at the heart of the multiethnic church), organizing our churches around people just like ourselves weakens our impact on and connection to the culture around us. If Jesus came "to seek and to save that which was lost" (Luke 19:10 NASB), then surely he came to save the lostness of humans in the context of their relationships toward each other.

What we see in Ephesians 3 is that God does not have an organizing principle of homogeneity at the center of his gospel mission. Literally, the kind of church Christ came to reveal is just the opposite. Understandably, depending on the diversity found in the location of a church, not all churches can fully embody God's diverse heart or in the exact same way as another church. When a city or nation is homogenous in some way, then the church of Jesus will reflect that reality! Paul's point is not that every church must be diverse in every way possible but that, because of Jesus, God's church should accept no ethnic, classist, or racial boundaries. We need not honor the confines of "the most segregated hour," as Dr. Martin Luther King Jr. famously critiqued on *Meet the Press* in 1960.[5]

Under the microscope of Ephesians 3, we understand the body of Christ contains nonhomogeneous DNA—and Paul showed he was willing to sacrifice to maintain it. What about us?

---

[5] Martin Luther King Jr., "Meet the Press," YouTube, April 17, 1960, https://www.youtube.com/watch?v=1q881g1L_d8.

MORGAN

Immeasurably More than We Ask or Think

Recently, I attended a chapel at a local Christian school. The school was honoring graduating seniors that day, and the head of the school shared an encouraging message at the end of the service. He spoke about how God would go with the students as they headed out into the world and how God was able to help them accomplish their dreams if they trusted him throughout their lives. It was an encouraging message, without question. Then he quoted this verse—the capstone of Ephesians 3— as the foundation of his talk:

> Now to him who is able to do immeasurably more than all we ask or imagine, according to his power that is at work within us, to him be glory in the church and in Christ Jesus throughout all generations, for ever and ever! Amen. (Eph. 3:20–21 NIV)

If you're like me or those students that day, you have heard Ephesians 3:20 quoted, oh, a few thousand times to bolster flagging faith: *don't give up; God is able; keep believing for that new car, new house, new spouse, better vacation.* It's the verse that has launched a thousand charismatic prayer meetings (and I have loved every one of them!).

However, while God does orchestrate miraculous circumstances to lead, heal, and care for his people, there are far better scriptures for those truths than Ephesians 3:20. The "immeasurably more than all we could ask or imagine" Paul referred to has nothing to do with God's abundant ability to provide for his people materially or smooth the path ahead for new graduates. It has everything to do with a new kind of people and church in the world; it has exclusively to do with "the mystery of Christ" revealed.

The immeasurable abundance of God that set Paul's heart ablaze was not a vision for a new car but a vision for a new people. After all, what takes immeasurably more faith to believe for: a new car, passing grades in your first semester of college, or witnessing the miraculous sight of all peoples of the world putting down their hate to love one another?

Paul understood that God had done immeasurably more than we will ever fully grasp when he sent his Son to redeem humanity from its sin. He realized Jesus's sacrifice would do immeasurably more than we can imagine if we will hold on to the mystery that somehow, as different as we all are, God has made us one with him and one in him.

When the world seems to have gone mad with power grabs and cultural fragmentation, we forget that the people of God are supposed to operate differently, set apart from the world's ways. When our relationships seem risky and the world seems unsafe, we need our friends around us to remind us that God has given us good news that provides "power that is at work within *us*" (Eph. 3:20 NIV—emphasis mine).

Everywhere he went, Paul never forgot that God deposits the power for *us* in diverse and life-changing friendships that fully express God's heart and carry God's mission into the world. A glance over at Romans 16 will lay to rest any question about Paul's commitment to diversity in his friendships. There, we find twenty-four verses full of the names of Paul's friends, and not many of the names are Jewish.

Everywhere he went, Paul was loving into the future, and the mystery power of diverse friendships helped him get there.

A Friend for the Whole World

We can find the mystery of Christ revealed in Eddie Jaku's words that one friend can become our whole world. Because our friend

Jesus has cared for us and loved us to the very end (John 13:1), if we look deeply into the love of Christ, we find that not only does our friend Jesus become our whole world, but in Jesus the whole world becomes our friend. Paul hinted at this truth when he wrote:

> So in Christ Jesus you are all children of God through faith, for all of you who were baptized into Christ have clothed yourselves with Christ. There is neither Jew nor Gentile, neither slave nor free, nor is there male and female, for you are all one in Christ Jesus. If you belong to Christ, then you are Abraham's seed, and heirs according to the promise. (Gal. 3:26–29 NIV)

Seeing Jesus as the redeemer and friend the world needs reveals how our lives as Christians can reflect the final image in the book of Ruth: joint heirs in the diverse family of God, gathered around our redeemer, singing his praises.

To strengthen the bonds of love in our spiritual family, we must offer Ruth's powerful words to as many people as possible: *Your people are my people; your God is my God; your family is my family.* To empower and rescue our family, we must offer Boaz's generosity to those in need: *Stay in my field; don't go away from here; I will redeem you; I will humble myself and pay the cost for you to be whole.* To comfort our family, we must wisely promise others what Naomi promised Ruth: *I want to find rest for your soul.* When words like these become the baseline and foundation of our relationships, God's mysterious power makes us his church and Christ's hands and feet in the world.

Truth be told, redemption isn't the result of more separation, selfishness, or keeping our eyes on our personal needs, wants, and preferences. We hope the story of Ruth inspires people to lift up their eyes and see how God worked through Boaz, Naomi, and Ruth. Their multigenerational, multiethnic, and socioeconomically unique friendship with one another birthed a vision beyond themselves that brought God's redemption into the world.

There have always been many valid reasons to fear the world is beyond repair. But God's love defies that fear, repelling cynicism and despair by making room for those who call upon the name of the Lord. When the darkness of hatred, injustice, and sin threatens to overwhelm us, 1 John 3 is good medicine for our souls:

> What marvelous love the Father has extended to us! Just look at it—we're called children of God! That's who we really are. But that's also why the world doesn't recognize us or take us seriously, because it has no idea who he is or what he's up to.
>
> But friends, that's exactly who we are: children of God. And that's only the beginning. Who knows how we'll end up! What we know is that when Christ is openly revealed, we'll see him—and in seeing him, become like him. All of us who look forward to his Coming stay ready, with the glistening purity of Jesus' life as a model for our own. (1 John 3:1–3 *The Message*)

This passage highlights that, no matter how earnestly the world attempts to understand how diversity and belonging comingle in Christ, without a deep understanding of God's marvelous love, they will never recognize his redemptive plans. It's no wonder, then, that when the world sees a diverse gathering of Christian believers, they might miss seeing that by our gospel-based clinging to one another, we prepare our hearts for the day we see our Savior face-to-face.

Love becomes a choice we repeatedly make as we model our lives after Jesus's. We do not love a diversity of people to elevate diversity as a cultural value; we love a diversity of people because that love makes us more Christlike.

Our Choice

A community of diverse gospel friendships is founded on the choice to love everyone we can now because God has destined us to love everyone who belongs to him in eternity.

On any given Sunday at our church, we choose to gather around our redeemer as Boaz, Ruth, and Naomi gathered around the baby who represented the future redeemer of Israel. In the rows of chairs sit old, young, rich, poor, single, and married people of every kind of ethnic background. We hold our friendships with one another as Naomi held Obed, cherishing the product of an unusual diverse union in our lap as we experience in this life a small piece of the redemption yet to come with Christ's return.

We repent and forgive when conflicts, misunderstandings, or ignorance threaten to weaken the bonds created by Christ's love in our friendships. We lament and celebrate together to strengthen those bonds. We try, in any way possible, to embody God's heart for one another so our lives will prove our love for God is real and true. After all, as John aptly wrote in 1 John 4:20, if we can't love the people we can see, how can we claim to love God, who is invisible to our eyes?

We hope to show the world Jesus's love for all people as we choose to worship in a community that honors God's diverse people, all of whom were made in his image. God's love compels us to pursue his missional heart to love and serve our city, plant churches, train leaders, and make disciples. We hear the voice of God speaking over anyone willing to follow him into risky relational waters saying, *Well done, good and faithful servants.* We hear the voice of God cheering those who have carried the banner of the "mystery of Christ": *You have been faithful with little; I am going to trust you with more.* We hear him saying to those who have suffered through decades of trials caused by building bridges across the fault lines of culture, *Your work is great, the labor is wearying, and the cost is steep—but as you sacrifice and give, my fire will fall and bring redemption to many so that the world will see who I am.*

And we pray this over the future: May God's never-ending love rise up to meet you when your hope or faith wearies. May that love lead you to people you can cling to on the long journey ahead, and may God cause others to cling to you so you will never face the road ahead alone. May your heart remember that although you are a stranger and a foreigner here, a reward awaits you in God's eternal presence.

And may your friendships lead you to the one and only God, whose love can save the world.

ACKNOWLEDGMENTS

As we consider the subject matter of this book, we've realized the impossibility of naming all the friends whose perspectives, generosity, courage, rebukes, forgiveness, and grace have made the words on these pages possible. What we have shared about friendship and diversity is the fruit of all we have learned from our own friends. We have been blessed with countless wonderful people who love us well, and for that we are grateful. However, we will try to name a few key groups and people, but if you are our friend and you don't find your name here, please know you are in our hearts and we will try to make it up to you with Tex-Mex some night.

To Terrance, KH, Joslin, Rosalynn, Lorena, Keong, Leah, Meagan, Carla, and Jack: We suspect the stories you shared in this book will be the pages readers are most blessed to read. Your words are so full of God's deep love that Carrie cried as she read them. (This is a fact that will shock no one, of course.) Thank you for trusting us with your stories; but even more, thank you for being our friends.

To John and Gaylen: While your sacrifice and love for God's people as elders at Mosaic will only ever be fully understood by God himself, please know we are continually in awe of you. It's a joy and privilege to call you our friends.

To Mosaic Church: We offer our gratitude for giving us the chance to shoot for the moon and attempt the impossible task of pastoring a church. You proved your kindness to us when you forgave Morgan for that time he rode a bike up into the pulpit on a Sunday morning and when you voted for Carrie in the Christmas Eve chili cook-off in 2011 (it was straight out of the can, y'all). We love you to the very end.

To the amazing people who make up the Mosaic Church staff team, past and present: Thank you for loving God and everyone else so courageously. We wouldn't want to do any of this without you guys. Easter potlucks for life!

To Every Nation Churches and Ministries: Thank you for believing that changing the campus can change the world. Your faithfulness to plant campus ministries changed our lives forever, and we feel honored to be a part of such a diverse, global spiritual family.

To Jude, Jack, Jase, and Finley: You amaze us in new ways all the time. Please play more foosball with your father, and don't forget to call your mom.

To our parents: Thank you for staying married and showing us what commitment looks like. You're a blessing in our lives!

To Morgan's sometimes five, sometimes six guys: Please forgive him for the near-death experience in the woods. He meant well.

To Brett, Melissa, Kevin, and Jody: You already know this, but we'd be lost without you guys. Please, let's actually take that trip to the beach or the mountains someday soon. This all talk and no action thing must end!

To our agent, Mary DeMuth, and Leafwood Publishers: Thank you for believing in us and this book. It means more than you know.

Certainly, we ultimately owe everything to God, including this book. Jesus, you are our first and most faithful friend; thank you for saving us. Holy Spirit, we pray you will make much of our words despite all the ways these pages fail to properly communicate your unfathomable love for us all. Father, we hope our lives honor your heart for the world and bring you glory.